WOMAN LET GO

Release the Grip of Unforgiveness

Karen
McCracken

ISBN 978-0-9893158-4-5
Woman Let Go ©
womaninspired.com/Karen McCracken
2024 All rights reserved.

Portions of this book were taken from
The Woman Inspired Podcast, © 2023
All rights reserved. Edited by Inspired
Editing Services, 2024

Dedication

This book is from my heart, for God's glory. For every time I've been hurt, rejected, dismissed, and devalued, He has reminded me I am loved. Through His amazing example of grace, He has prompted me to be a forgiver of others, and of myself. All glory, credit, honor and praise to Him.

He has saved me from my iniquity, my flaws, and my desire to control that which I cannot control. No matter the mistakes I've made or wrongs I've been unable to right, He has graciously, compassionately, come alongside me, filled me with His love, and blessed me with forgiveness that I do not deserve.

By Jesus Christ's passionate example of forgiveness, I've come to embrace the truth that every Christian's quest to be Christ-like absolutely cannot be fulfilled without releasing the grip that unforgiveness has over our lives.

For those who hold on to unforgiveness, this book is for you. My hope and prayer is that within these pages you find the hope and help you need in order to let go.

♡ Karen

Contents

Introduction

"Forgiveness is a powerful expression of the love within our soul." - Anthony Douglas

When someone asked me why I speak about forgiveness so much, I read them that quote from Anthony Douglas. I believe wholeheartedly that forgiveness is a powerful expression of the love we carry within us, born from the acceptance of Jesus Christ into our lives. It's an expression of the love you have for Jesus Christ, who himself was the ultimate, passion-driven example of forgiveness and grace. When we forgive others we honor Jesus and His commandment to us to forgive. Within the obedient act of forgiveness also lies the truth that in order to be Christ-like, we absolutely must forgive others.

Forgiveness is powerful because it's an expression of our faith and a manifestation of the grace Jesus has deposited inside each of us, but also because it has the power to free us. Forgiveness frees us from the grip of disobedience, guilt, and fear. It may seem like a small thing but the power that forgiveness holds can change not just our own lives but the lives of those we ultimately forgive. On the flip side of that same coin lives unforgiveness. Unforgiveness itself is an act of disobedience towards Jesus Christ and the Word of God. It also holds great power. It has the power to weigh us down, trap us, create mental and emotional anguish, and keep us from the path we were meant to walk while on this earth.

Over the past 24 years of speaking, teaching, and writing, one of the constant themes I find in the lives of those I've been blessed to minister to is the struggle to forgive others and yet, we have the greatest example of forgiveness and sacrifice there's ever been through the sacrifice Jesus Christ made to forgive each of us of our sins. Our human struggle to forgive others and ourselves is no accident. The forces of evil want nothing more than to create a culture of unforgiveness and all the pain it reaps. The world wants us to believe that we shouldn't get mad, we should just get even. It wants us to serve up a dish of revenge, bitterness, and anger that nothing can stop. The truth is though, that Jesus Christ and His Word can stop the grip of unforgiveness and the destructive domino effect it can have in our lives.

We were never meant to live a life of guilt and self-destruction but of conviction, repentance, and grace. Within these chapters lies a path and a process to forgiving others and forgiving self. Whether the unforgiveness you hold is towards someone who hurt you, abused you, used you, lied to you, lied about you, or rejected you, forgiveness can be given. Whether the forgiveness you seek is forgiving yourself or forgiving others, the strength you need to do so is available through Jesus.

My hope and prayer is that the insights, stories,

scriptures, quotes, and processes I share within these pages, given to me by a gracious and loving God, will also move you, prompt you, and inspire you to set out on a journey to forgive. I hope you will accept the challenge to forgive and be determined not to take it back.

My prayer for you is that you won't become focused on the size of the book, the picture on the front, the time it took to be shipped to you, or a typo the editing missed, but instead on the content of this book. My prayer is that as you sit down to read and digest, you'll grab a highlighter, paper, and a pen so you can take notes, take it to heart, and take it all straight to the Lord. If you're living a life gripped by unforgiveness and all the consequences that come with it, I pray you will soon let go and embrace what it feels like to release the grip of unforgiveness.

Karen

To find Karen's podcast, go to
womaninspired.com or search for
The Woman Inspired Podcast in your favorite
podcast player

WHAT IS FORGIVENESS?

Forgiveness seems like a simple concept, right? Someone tells you they're sorry, you say you forgive them, you move on. But that's not usually the way it happens. Because it doesn't often happen that way, the gaps in our understanding of just what it is and what it is not has left room for the world and Satan to squeeze in alternative ideas of what it means to forgive and whether or not we should forgive in the first place.

Much of the modern world is double-minded when it comes to the topic of forgiveness. We're told, especially in religious circles, that we should forgive and forget, let go, move on, and of course, if we do so then our personal success will be the best revenge against those who have hurt us. On the other hand, we're taught through social media, movies, and books, that forgiving is a sign of weakness. We're supposed to never forgive, hold someone accountable, or call them out on every public format available to us. Society has made it a common practice to be armed and ready to videotape anything they find unjust, unforgivable, and against societal propriety so they can spread that video all over the place. Sadly, people feel justified in doing so. How many times have you heard someone on social media or in a movie or perhaps a popular song talk about how they've been wronged and will never, ever forgive that other person? Or how they've been hurt and they're going to seek revenge?

There's a different way to live in this world that embraces unforgiveness. There's a way, a reason, and a purpose in forgiving others. Your forgiveness of another person is not for their benefit, although it might end up benefiting them in some way or another. Your forgiveness of someone may not seem possible yet it is. In fact, it's not just possible or probable; if you're a Christian it's expected.

Matthew 6:14-15 says, "If you forgive those who sin against you, your heavenly Father will forgive you. But if you refuse to forgive others, your Father will not forgive your sins."

This scripture is what prompts some people to at least attempt to forgive others and moves

Christians to feel guilty if they do not. Often, people just can't seem to wrap their brains around forgiveness and so they withhold it. Or they think they've forgiven someone and then they take it back later when something triggers the memory of what happened. After years of speaking to people about forgiveness and working on my own journey to maintain a forgiving attitude, I realized that numerous people sincerely don't know what forgiveness is. So, I'd like to start off these many pages that my heart has poured into by defining just what forgiveness is and what it is not.

According to Miriam Webster, forgiving means "To stop feeling anger toward someone or something; to cease to feel resentment against someone or something and to pardon." To pardon is defined as "the excusing of an offense without exacting a penalty." That's what Jesus did for us. He forgave us. He excused us, without exacting a penalty. He took the penalty for us.

Forgiving does not mean condoning someone else's actions or your own if you're the one who committed the transgression. Forgiving is not forgetting what someone did to you or what you did. (Forgiving and forgetting are two different things and we'll get into that in another chapter.) Forgiveness is not giving a stamp of approval. Forgiveness also doesn't mean that you have to forgive a person and then agree to have them in your life. If you were in a situation where someone hurt you and that hurt seems unforgivable, please understand that whatever IT is, absolutely is not unforgivable, and holding on to unforgiveness only hurts you in the long run.

Letting unforgiveness put you in a vice grip eventually hurts your relationship with the Lord because it's an act of disobedience. Disobedience creates a barrier between you and the Lord so refusing to forgive also hurts you. When we hold on to unforgiveness it often creates spiritual, physical, and mental issues that must be addressed. In the book of John Jesus tells us that if we love Him we will be obedient.

John 14:15-16, "If you love me, obey my commandments. And I will ask the Father, and he will give you another advocate, who will never leave you."

When we are obedient to His commandments, He brings us an advocate. Forgiveness is not a suggestion or an option. It's a commandment to us even though it's not listed on the stone tablets Moses brought down from the mountain.

That advocate Jesus was referring to in **John 14** was the Holy Spirit. We have the presence of the Holy Spirit to help us through the pain but also through the forgiveness process and to help us continue to obey the command to forgive. We could have no better help than that of the Holy Spirit and yet we forget that fact in the middle of our hurt, anger, and resentment. When we work to obey, blessings come out of it. It's a difficult thing to remember when we're in the midst of the struggle to let go of unforgiveness that is painful and harsh. That's why it's so important to learn it and hold on to the lessons and the truth that the Holy Spirit will not leave us. He will be here to advocate for us time and again as we work to obediently forgive.

Forgiving a person does not mean you have to have them in your life and it doesn't even mean you have to face that person or tell them you have forgiven them. I've heard more than a handful of people who said they couldn't forgive someone because they didn't want to ever face them again. Forgiving is an internal, spiritual act, performed out of obedience, for your good, not for theirs. If the Lord prompts you to face them or moves you to vocalize that you have forgiven them or write them a letter or email them, then be obedient in that too, but facing someone who wronged you is not mandatory in order to forgive them.

Forgiving someone does not mean they have to apologize to you for you to forgive. The reality is there's a good chance they may never say they're sorry or even realize they have something to be sorry for. It was hard for me to accept this truth in my life. To comprehend that a person who has hurt you might never acknowledge that they hurt you is a hard pill to swallow. I was raised in a household where we were taught we had to acknowledge when we did something wrong and apologize for it or there were consequences. It's ingrained in me to be apologetic. But the world at large has adopted the motto, "No apologies necessary". We have to remember that a person who hurt us may never understand they hurt us, simply for the fact that they may be selfish and narcissistic or because they're unaware of how hurtful they can be. Some people won't even acknowledge it, even if you try to tell them. Still others prefer to sit in denial rather than stay open to the fact that they need to work on themselves. These are the facts we have to face when we set out to have a forgiving spirit and be obedient to God's Word in **Matthew 6:14-15**. So please take note that a person who hurt you might never apologize to you but that doesn't mean you're released from the commandment to forgive.

There is a quote I read years ago that I love. While I never have been able to find out who coined it, I will share it nonetheless. It says, "I never knew how strong I was until I had to forgive someone who wasn't sorry and accept the apology I never got." - Uknown

Forgiving the wrongs that no one would apologize for or acknowledge adds another small layer of pain that can quickly turn to resentment if we don't deal with it. Distant hurts and pains we've tucked deep down inside due to unforgiveness, pretending we could move on from them, are also a challenge to dredge back up and seek to forgive but we still have the call on our lives to do just that. It's not an easy process for most of us but there are some steps I'll share with you that I hope help you on this journey to let go of the unforgiveness.

Sometimes we don't realize where we are in our forgiveness process or if we've actually forgiven someone or not because we have a distorted idea of what true forgiveness looks like. The world has taught us to fake it till we make it. Have you ever thought you've forgiven someone, and then later realized you haven't? You've just been faking it, not dealing with it, and pushing the feelings down? I have. I've been there. I've held on to unforgiveness in the past and it completely affected my health and my walk with the Lord.

Are you in the grip of unforgiveness? Not sure if you are? I've dissected the process I went through and come up with three signs that you're holding on to unforgiveness.

3 signs you're holding on to unforgiveness

Sign #1 - When you try to rest, your mind takes you to that person, that thing, or that action that you haven't forgiven. For me, I thought I'd forgiven someone who hurt me deeply. What I'd actually done was pretend the issue didn't exist. I didn't deal with her, talk to her, or see her, which was a healthy thing for me because she's a toxic person but still, I didn't deal with it on an emotional, mental, or spiritual level either. I just pretended the issue didn't exist. One day someone mentioned her to me and it triggered something deep inside. Suddenly I found myself thinking about her, about the things she said to me, and the ways she disregarded me and discarded me. Every time after that when I tried to lay down at night or when I was really tired, she came to my mind again and the same old hurt rose up in me. I became angry, sad, and crying at the drop of a hat. I'd let the past and that hurt control my emotions yet again. I thought I had put all that behind me but what I'd actually done was push it further back in my mind, trying to pretend it never happened. I learned a tough lesson. When we "put it behind us", it usually means we have just pushed it behind all the other memories. But it's still there. We've hidden it beneath the expectations of what forgiveness looks like. I learned that if it's still taunting you, then you haven't forgiven.

I fell for the "forgive and forget" mantra the world tells us and when I realized I hadn't forgiven her and I couldn't forget it, I felt like a failure. I became angry at the world at large, taking it out on the people closest to me. In the process, I realized I was also angry at God for not taking the memory of the pain away from me. I tried to forgive. I tried to be obedient but I knew in that moment when I was triggered, feeling that familiar deep pain again, that I wasn't sure what forgiveness was. I started blaming God, getting angry at Him instead of praying to Him. Had I allowed myself to truly process the incidents and the pain; forgiving from the inside out, I would never have been triggered. Would I have remembered the wrongs and the person who perpetrated them on me when someone brought her up? Yes, I would have but I wouldn't have been held tight by the grip of unforgiveness.

I still remember the pain from this broken relationship with that toxic person but I don't live in it any longer. I don't weep over it or over her anymore. Unforgiveness doesn't have a grip on me and neither does the memory. God took all that from me when I was finally able to forgive her and with the power of His advocate, the Holy Spirit, I was comforted, renewed, and free from the burden of the pain of unforgiveness.

There's a quote I read during that difficult time that stuck with me. While the author is unknown, the quote is one I hope you'll write down and memorize. It says, "The most influential person in your life is the one you refuse to forgive." The person whom you allow to take up space in your mind is the one who shapes your decisions, your thoughts, and your daily emotional life. If that's someone who has hurt you, why are you allowing them to be such a great influence in your life and over your thoughts and feelings?

Again, your thought life and what you dwell on or are triggered by can be a great indicator of whether or not you're holding on to unforgiveness. Have you ever caught yourself trying to sleep at night or go for a walk, meditate, or pray and your brain goes straight into a scenario where you confront that person who hurt you? In your scenario, you tell them all the things you wish you had but never did. That person is or is close to becoming the most influential person in your life. Does your brain make up scenarios where you can chew them out, confront them, or even get revenge? Then they are still influencing you. If the person and events you have not forgiven are still influencing you or controlling your emotions and thought processes, you have not forgiven them.

Sign # 2 – You haven't let go of the anger you

feel towards that person or perhaps towards yourself for 'allowing' yourself to get hurt. Remember the definition of forgiveness is "Ceasing to resent, to stop feeling anger; to pardon." If you find yourself talking about that person or that hurt over and over again then you haven't forgiven them. They are still influencing you. Do you hash it out, rehash it out, repeat it to your close friends, your family, and even to God? Do you find you're seething deep down inside when you hear that person's name or someone else brings up that person and boom, anger suddenly rises up, spilling over into your thoughts and actions yet again? That's a sign that you're holding on to unforgiveness.

I have a relative who was deeply hurt by her husband and even though it was 30 years ago, she still talks about it. She admittedly says she still holds resentment and yet she says she's forgiven him. The very first sign of him doing the slightest thing wrong today, like perhaps forgetting to take out the trash, or not doing the dishes the way she wanted and she gets angry with him. When she gets angry she brings up that past situation from 30 years ago and uses it against him. When she's angry with him she calls people she knows and tells them all about it. That is unforgiveness.

Sign #3 – Making insults, participating in negative gossip, and derogatory comments. What do I mean by that? The person you've been hurt by becomes the target of your insults, bullying, negative talk, cussing, and gossip. When you hear their name you fling out an insult or negative remark about them. Even when you don't hear their name but that person is on your mind, you bring them up as the butt of your jokes and sarcasm. You fling out insults about them and harp on the negative things about him or her at random.

I know a man who got a divorce after his wife had become addicted to over-the-counter pain meds. That addiction turned into an illegal drug addiction. She refused to get help and she eventually started sleeping with other men for money so she could buy drugs without the loss of money being detected from their bank accounts. She ended up divorcing him and she left the 2 kids with him, rarely showing up for visits. Naturally, being a Christian, he said he had forgiven her but in the middle of playing a card game at a family party he might suddenly come out with some joke or comment that made fun of her or insulted her. He'd often say things like, "I have to take out the garbage. Oh wait, she already left me, never mind." Then he'd laugh. While it might have seemed funny and some people would laugh that uncomfortable, sad laugh that happens when someone makes remarks like that, it really wasn't funny. It was a clear sign that he hadn't forgiven her. He was naturally still hurting and grieving but his anger, insults, and constant bringing her up into his conversation were signs that he hadn't forgiven her.

Often when we're on a quest to forgive someone, we also go through grief because many times that person we're trying to forgive is someone we know and love. Whether that person stays in our life or doesn't, a loss has been had on some level. Trust may have been lost. The depth of the relationship may have changed. The intimacy you had with someone may be gone or the entire relationship may have been lost. So, unless the person you're forgiving is a stranger or a mere acquaintance, we often experience grief in the middle of trying to forgive. That grief includes the common stages of grief, which are denial, anger, bargaining, depression, and acceptance. A clear sign that unforgiveness is present is when someone is stuck in the denial and anger stage of grief over the change in the relationship or loss of it, much like the man whose wife left him and the kids.

The insults, negative talk, and derogatory comments can also be about yourself when you haven't forgiven yourself for something. Do you find yourself saying you're stupid, worthless, or ignorant? Maybe, just maybe you're holding on to some unforgiveness towards yourself and that unforgiveness has chipped away at your self-esteem as well as your relationship with God. Harboring unforgiveness tends to knock us off the path we're supposed to be on. I've been there. It can be challenging to take our thoughts captive and stop the negative self-talk but going through the process of identifying if we're holding on to unforgiveness and then actually working to forgive makes all the difference in the world. It makes a difference in how you feel about yourself and most definitely in your closeness to the Lord.

When it comes down to it, no matter who you are, how old you are, or what you've been through, when you hold on to unforgiveness you're holding on to something that binds you up, slowly wraps you in chains and steals your peace. Unforgiveness creates a place in our minds for resentment, bitterness, and anger to grab hold and stick. Whether the anger comes from grief or the natural reaction to being hurt, we must be diligent not to let it grow and build a dangerous stronghold within our minds. Where there is resentment, bitterness, and anger, there is no peace. There is little room in our lives to rest, rejuvenate, or realign ourselves with God's calling if we're taking up that time and space by holding on to resentment and anger that comes from not forgiving. That alone will create a separation between you and Jesus Christ.

Woman of God, Let Go:

- Do you know if you're holding on to unforgiveness? Some people do. Instantly when the topic of forgiveness is brought up, they know who and what they haven't forgiven. Some of us even justify it by saying, "If God wanted me to forgive, He would have made a way for me to do that already." Well, now is your time. He's making a way now. If you already know of people you haven't forgiven then start making your list so you can go through the process it takes to finally forgive.

- Are you unsure if you're harboring unforgiveness and yet, see the signs that perhaps you are? Take the time to write down people you believe you have forgiven and pray over each one to make sure you're not harboring unforgiveness. Take it to the Lord in prayer. As you do, in quiet prayerful time, go over each one and analyze it through the lens of the "3 signs you're holding on to unforgiveness" I shared in this chapter. Take notes if needed. Let God show you if and where you're harboring unforgiveness so you can work through the process of forgiving.

- Consider the truth in this quote: "The most influential person in your life is the one you refuse to forgive." If there's someone who's taking up more time, space, thought, and emotion in your life other than Jesus, then pray for the Holy Spirit to show you why. Seek the Lord for release from the unforgiveness that has undue influence over your daily life.

WHAT DID JESUS SAY ABOUT FORGIVENESS?

Several places in the Bible reference forgiveness. For this chapter, we're going to get to the crux of what Jesus said about forgiveness through what are likely the most quoted Bible verses on the subject.

"Then Peter came to him and asked, "Lord, how often should I forgive someone who sins against me? Seven times?", "No, not seven times," Jesus replied, "but seventy times seven!" Matthew 18:21-22

The Bible says clearly here in **Matthew 18: 21- 22** that Peter had a conversation with Jesus and asked him if he must forgive someone who sins against him, even up to seven times? While I knew the Bible said that, when I felt the need to dig more into forgiveness I read it again and I could just hear my son's voice in my head reacting to that type of an answer. An incredulous sounding, "What? I have to forgive that many times? You've got to be kidding me!" I imagine that might have been Peter's reaction as well. But Jesus tells Peter more than that. He says, "Not just seven times but seventy times seven." In some translations of the Bible, they've changed this passage to state seventy-seven times but some translations clearly state seventy times seven. That's not just seventy-seven times we're told to forgive but four hundred ninety times. Many Biblical scholars believe that the original language meant seventy times seven, while others believe that the exact numbers actually make no difference. *

The number seven is known in Hebrew as a number signifying perfection, which many believe reflects the significance of forgiveness. The fact that the scripture most likely says seventy times seven is also significant. Seventy times seven is four hundred ninety. I used to joke and say, "Hey, if I only have to forgive four hundred ninety times, that means I get to smack someone the four hundred ninety-first time, right?" I think some people can relate to that desire. We all have times we want to retaliate, lash out, or get even and while I still giggle about that thought, it strikes me just how specific Jesus' answer was. He could have chosen any number or set of numbers but he chose these. Some people believe he used the number seven frequently because it is considered the number of perfection in the Bible. God rested on the seventh day. There are seven churches in the book of Revelation as well as seven seals, seven bowls, seven trumpets, and many more references in the Bible to the number seven surrounding the return of Jesus Christ.

When you read the Bible, throughout it there are some very specific instructions. The Bible describes things in the Old and New Testament down to the smallest detail. From the number of cubits high that Noah was supposed to build the arc all the way through to the very detailed events in Revelation, we see that what we were given was precise. We're given the information we need to know to live the life we were given, including how and what to do, and what to expect. We just have to be willing to study it, seek strength to be obedient to it, and embrace living the way the Lord has called us to live. If we do this, it's easy to see that He always has our best interests in mind. How He calls us to forgive is no different.

When I first read that I needed to forgive someone four hundred ninety times I thought that would be easy because that's a fairly high number. When it sunk in that I probably have to ask the Lord's forgiveness for my own transgressions at least four hundred ninety times in one week, I realized that it actually was not such a high number. Think about how easy it is to accumulate four hundred ninety or more sins just in your thought-life alone and having to take each of those to the foot of the cross to repent. It made me ache inside as I became keenly aware that I could never count high enough nor know what a tremendously large number of sins Jesus died for when He was crucified for us. Can you fathom how many sins he took on? What was the spiritual and emotional weight that He carried as He sacrificed and died for us? My sins alone are enough to weigh a man down. Yours are enough. But they weren't just yours and mine. He forgave and still forgives far more than seventy times seven for each of us. That truth made me realize that what He is asking me to do by forgiving others is small in comparison to what He has already done for us.

When Jesus died for us, he died so that we could be forgiven, and pardoned. He pardoned us without exacting a punishment on us. He was a living sacrifice and atonement for our wrongs. His grace knows no bounds. There's a song whose lyrics go, "Grace, grace, God's grace; grace that is greater than all our sins." Not just some of our sins but all of them. His grace is greater than your sins and even the person whose sins you don't think should be forgiven. He is able to forgive anyone who comes to Him. The person who hurt you, the family member who lied to you, the drug dealer who got your child hooked, the pastor who broke your confidence, the church member who gossiped about you, the sister who rejected you, the spouse who cheated on you, the person in front of you at Kroger who has fifty-five items in the twenty items or less lane! All of them. Jesus died for all these people's sins, including yours. His grace surpassed death, into eternal life, and on that cross, He said "It is finished'.

When Jesus died on the cross, His last words being "It is finished" meant that He was done with our sins. He isn't holding those transgressions against us. When He forgave, He forgave and it was finished. When the topic of forgiveness became a big part of my life I had to dig into what it really meant because what I wanted more than anything was to be able to say that I had forgiven and I was done with it. I didn't want to keep revisiting the pain and grief, feeling as if I had forgiven and then taking it back when I got upset again. I didn't want to pull up reminders and scenarios in my head of what I had relentlessly held on to. I wanted to be released once and for all from the grip of unforgiveness.

The way my brain works propels me to want to know the background, the root words, and the true meaning of things if at all possible because then I feel as if I can properly apply them. It's no different with the commandment to forgive. When I had lived for several years easily forgiving the little things and yet I became anxious and emotional all the time, I realized how much holding on to the unforgiveness of the bigger hurts in my life was affecting me. Holding onto what I would consider the larger transgressions caused me so much deep emotional pain.

I eventually sought counseling for those hurts and pains. Counseling isn't necessary for everyone but for me, seeing a Christian counselor to help me identify why I was so anxious illuminated my need to forgive rather than staying on the treadmill of pain that kept me in a pattern of just pretending to forgive. I'd learned the art of slapping on a smiley-face mask for the world; all the while I pushed my unforgiveness deeper to the back of my mind. Doing all that only worked for so long and then the consequences of holding on to the unforgiveness started to leak out into other areas of my life. I liken it to dumping toxic waste in a beautiful yard and covering it up with a pile of leaves so no one knows it's there. Eventually, the toxic waste will start killing the beautiful foliage around it. Nothing good can grow because what's underneath is killing it. I had toxic unforgiveness that I'd tried to cover up with a heap of autumn leaves and it was starting to kill me. Covering it up, and pushing it back so it was supposedly behind me didn't work. Eventually, all those things you push into the back of your mind so you don't have to deal with them come out in one form or another.

When I finally stopped listening to the world tell me how to forgive and sought the Word of God and His direction, it changed everything. I wanted to live a life where unforgiveness no longer had a grip on me. I did the research I needed to do so I could get it right. I took the time in prayer, listening to the promptings of Jesus and the Holy Spirit. My very physical, emotional, mental, and spiritual health depended on me letting go of the unforgiveness. And more importantly, as I came to understand it, the One who took on my sins and forgave me, deserved for me to be obedient to what He said I should do.

In my researching, I dug into the meaning of forgiveness. In order to share with you what I found out I have to tell you briefly and as simply as possible a little bit about the Hebrew language. For those who are unfamiliar, Hebrew is an alphanumeric language. That basically means that every letter and every word has a numeric value. For example, if we did that in English it might be that A equals 1, B equals 2, etc. The Hebrew language is made up then of numbers and letters. Each number has a definition and meaning to it as do the letters and groupings of numbers and letters. Groups of words and numbers together might have a deeper meaning than what we would give our individual English words. The words from the scripture in Matthew about forgiveness from Jesus to Peter are no different.

Jesus said to forgive even seventy times seven. Seventy times seven equals four hundred ninety. Four hundred ninety is the numerical value of the Hebrew word "tamim" (sounds like taw-meem), which in Hebrew means "completed or finished." It's used in Hebrew to denote something that is fully completed, finished, and is no more. **

When the truth of what four hundred ninety means sunk in, all I could do was cry. On and off for hours, pouring myself out to the Lord, I asked Him to help me to forgive and I praised Him for showing me what I needed to know. This one principle forever changed the way I see forgiveness and grace. It also drove home the immense significance in Jesus' final words on the cross when he said, "It is finished." In His words to Peter, He was telling us that when we forgive we are to forgive and be finished with it. Now when I take something to Him and ask for forgiveness, I think about the deep pain I feel when I'm going through the process of forgiving and I can't help but weep at the knowledge that the pain He endured was literally so much greater than that because He took on ALL our sins and forgave each of us who go to Him to seek that forgiveness. My quest to forgive like Jesus and say "it is finished" is greater than it's ever been.

While Jesus' primary language would have been Aramaic, He would also have been fluent in Hebrew. The significance in Jesus' very specific words to Peter as He told him to forgive seventy times seven (four hundred ninety), making it "finished", hits me to the core of who I am every time I read that scripture. When we forgive we're supposed to forgive and not take it back. We're to be finished with it. Be finished with that person negatively affecting us, finished with that hurt, that pain; that unforgiveness. We're supposed to let that issue, that anger, that resentment be finished in our lives. Let it be finished controlling us, gripping us with fear, anger, grief, "what if's", and thoughts of revenge.

Nothing is random in God's Word. While it might seem that Jesus pulled out an odd random number of times we're supposed to forgive, what many theologians and Biblical scholars – Jewish and Christian alike – believe is that Jesus was indeed saying to Peter that we are to forgive and say it is finished. Just as Jesus forgave; once and for all, we're to do the same. Let your act of forgiveness allow you to finish with your strife, your pain, your holding it against someone else. Let your act of forgiveness remove the worry over that person and that issue. Let it be finished.

Let it be four hundred ninety. Do not forgive and take it back but say it is finished. **

After studying this, I decided I needed a reminder of this principle so I made myself a bracelet that says "It is finished" on one side and "Keepin' it 490" on the other. I'm forgiving and I'm not taking it back.

No longer be held captive by unforgiveness

Jesus clearly called us to be obedient; to forgive, with Him as the ultimate example of such forgiveness. Jesus wants us to no longer be held captive to unforgiveness but instead, He wants us to allow the grip of it to be released from our lives. That's how we let go. We let it go to Jesus, out of love and obedience to Him.

In researching the significance of four hundred ninety and the Hebrew word tamim (taw-meem), I found that tamim is also means whole-hearted and complete. If you overlay this deeper meaning of the word onto the process of true forgiveness, the significance of Jesus' response to Peter in Matthew is even deeper. When we hold on to unforgiveness it breaks us. When we truly give a four hundred ninety type of forgiveness we have no choice but to do so whole-heartedly or we won't be finished with it.***

It could also be said that Christ was referring here

to the four hundred ninety years that the Jews had spent in captivity. They were enslaved and in the four hundred ninetieth year they were set free. Again, numeric values and meanings are significant in the Hebrew language and culture. This wasn't just the way Jesus spoke. It was the way everyone in that time period and culture spoke. Some scholars and theologians also believe that the reference to forgiveness is a reminder to us that at the four hundred ninetieth year the captives were set free. When we forgive to the fullness of seventy times seven, we are no longer held captive by unforgiveness and all it chains us to. When we forgive in the mindset and obedience of seventy times seven, the grip of unforgiveness has been released and, praise Jesus, we are set free. ****

Woman of God, Let Go:

- Take time to read and pray over **Matthew 18:21-22**. Ask the Lord to shine the light on where you've forgiven and then taken it back. Keep notes so you can work through the process of forgiving once and for all. As you know you've forgiven, take a marker and black out that transgression, looking at it no more. No longer keep a record of it on paper or in the back of your mind. Let the Lord show you how to release the grip that unforgiveness has had on you.

- On some index cards, slips of paper, or on the back of some prayer cards, write down, "It is finished – Keepin' in 490". Put one in your Bible, one in your purse, one on your bathroom mirror, on the dash of your car, on your fridge and anyplace else you'll see it on a regular basis. When I'm having a day where past transgressions from others or myself come creeping back at me, I put on my Keepin' it 490 bracelet because it reminds me not to pick that forgiveness up and turn it back into unforgiveness. God does not ask us to do that which we are incapable of doing. While it takes effort, it's totally possible. We usually need His help doing it and most likely you will need practice, but it IS possible to forgive and say "It is finished".

Note: Keepin' it 490 bracelets are available at all my speaking engagements. See my website at womaninspired.com for an events calendar or click the social media links on the website to connect with me there.

---

*Hermeneutics resource referencing the difference between 70 times 7, 77, 490 and the references to the book of Matthew. https://hermeneutics.stackexchange.com/questions/2443/why-is-there-numerical-ambiguity-in-matthew-1821-22

**References and resources on the Hebrew word tamim and 490:

1.
https://www.fusionglobal.org/connections/why-7-times-70/

2.
https://despisedsamaritan.com/2020/03/03/seventy-times-seven-the-forgiveness-dilemma/

*** 1.
https://www.hebrew4christians.com/Meditations/Tamim/tamim.html

**** 1. https://jewsforjesus.org/messianic-prophecies/the-messiah-would-come-according-to-a-timetable

KAREN MCCRACKEN

FORGET ABOUT THE FORGETTING

Sadly, if you hear some people talk about people like myself, (maybe you're one of those people like myself) you'll hear them say we're weak-minded push-overs because we forgive too easily. I must confess that there was a time when I was a pushover. I wasn't a pushover because I forgave easily but because I kept myself on a delusional quest to forgive and forget. You know, working to fulfill what the world says about forgiveness. It comes at us with mixed messages. It says we should forgive and forget and yet, it says that some things are unforgivable. The world also tells us not to get mad but to get even. The world, and our demonic adversaries, want nothing more than to see us fall for the quest to get even. Satan wants us to hold a grudge, retaliate, and stay in a pit of constant unforgiveness. That's why we're told again and again to "forget about it", even though that's not possible. I believe Satan planted the seeds of the "forgive and forget" philosophy as well as the "don't get mad, get even" mindset. The attempt to forget, or more precisely, pretend to forget, was the particular part that made me weak. The obedient action of forgiving didn't.

After years of letting other people walk all over me as I pretended to forget their transgressions, I now feel as if I should wear a banner over my head that says "Don't mistake my kindness and forgiveness for weakness." Through the Lord, I am strong. I believe in the verse from **Isaiah 40:29** which says **"He gives strength to the weary and increases the power of the weak."** In my process to forgive more completely without falling for the lies about what forgiveness is and isn't, I memorized that verse.

Many of us have bought into the lie that we have to forgive and forget. I used to believe that too and that's where people saw the weakness in me. They chalked it up to me forgiving too easily but that's not what it was. That's just what it looked like on the outside because, like me, so many others believe the same lie — that in order to forgive, you must also forget. I would act as if I forgot a transgression because I didn't know how to actually eliminate the memory of it from my mind or control when or how that memory may pop up. I could no more control that memory and pain from springing up than I could the memory of the pain I had when I broke my leg. That painful memory popped into my head for years every time I put on snow boots to walk out in the yard. Those boots, along with that beautiful cold, fluffy white stuff falling from the sky usually brings me joy but for a long time, it also brought me fear. I had a fear of repeating my fall in the snow and breaking my leg in three places. A snowy day is something I've learned to enjoy again but the memory of falling, while it no longer causes me anxiety and fear, it causes me to be cautious. As I recall the mistakes I made that day, including going out ill-prepared, wearing thin pajama pants, and improper footwear, I check myself to make sure I don't repeat those same mistakes. The smell of snow, the sound of a snow plow, and the sight of my winter boots all remind me of that day. That's not a choice I have. Were I to try and forget that incident, it would be impossible. But in remembering, I also recall the blessings that came out of that experience as well as the lessons I learned.

Were I to try and forget some of the traumatic, hurtful events in my life and the people who perpetrated those things, it would be impossible. Yet, that's what I was told to do. That's exactly what so much of the world believes should be done. Well, most likely half the world believes that. (I don't have valid statistics to back that up.

That's just my estimation from life experiences.) The other half seemingly thinks we should seek revenge and retaliate. But for the most part, and especially in Christian environments, we're still told to forgive and forget.

How many times have you been told to just let it all go, move on, quit dwelling on it? As if you can snap your fingers and erase the memory of something or someone that hurt you? In other words, just pretend. Be fake, smack on a mask, dull the pain, drink till it doesn't hurt, drug yourself up, get lost in binge-watching a show, or use the old standby of stuffing the memory as far back into the recesses of your mind as it will go. That's what so many people end up doing in a quest to try to forget.

Some people have actually forgiven but they've never forgotten and now they hold themselves to some standard that perpetually taunts them with the "forgive and forget" mantra. People try to forget because they believe that's what they're supposed to do. Forgiveness may be easy for some people but not all. Some people have accomplished it and then feel guilty when they remember the transgression as if remembering it means they've failed at forgiving. They then believe they have never forgiven merely because their human brain wouldn't let them forget it. They no longer feel that anger or grief from it but they just cannot forget the incident they had to forgive. So, come heck or high water, come high blood pressure or heart issues, come nightmares and breakdowns or addiction and dependency, they will work their hardest to attempt to force their brain to forget what they have already forgiven OR at the very least, attempt to forget it, even if they never forgave the person in the first place. Because then, at least they "forgot" and were obedient. It briefly, intermittently, gives them a sense of peace about it. Sadly, that peace doesn't last.

Does the Bible say to forgive and forget?

The Bible actually doesn't say we are supposed to forgive and forget. It's a human assumption that with forgiveness comes the ability to forget. Why? Because if we simply forget the sin then we can't hold it against someone. We can't. It's forgotten. Done, out of the brain, never to rub the hurt and wrongdoing in someone else's face or hold it against them. But think for a moment. If we did forget, that then eliminates the whole need to forgive in the first place. Doesn't it? It pretty much lets us off the hook. We don't have to do the work it takes to forgive, to heal, to maybe even help someone else through a similar forgiveness journey, or learn anything from the situation whatsoever if all we have to do is forget about it. We have brains that are made to remember for a reason. While I can't remember if I put the milk in the fridge or in the pantry at times, I actually cannot forget when someone hurt me, lied to me, abused me, cheated on me, or snubbed me. When there is a deep emotional reaction to an event or situation, it causes us to remember those things more easily and for longer.

Yes, I do realize that as we grow older we tend to forget things but that's a completely different principle. That's not a choice. That is a physiological and brain aging side-effect for many of us as we get older. I'm at that age now when my memory decides to occasionally go on hiatus for a while. One day I was talking to my aunt on the phone, all the while trying to gather things up to head out of the house. I was putting things in tote bags, looking for my To Do list but I couldn't find something I needed. I searched and searched and was getting incredibly frustrated. She must have heard it in my grunts and groans because she asked, "What's going on with you?" I said, "Grrr, I need to get on the road but I can't find my cell phone." She said, "You're talking on it." Those types of forgetfulness aren't what I'm referring to. While I can't remember where my phone is sometimes when it's right in my hand, I can remember the hurt feelings, the wrong-doings, and most everything others have done to cause me pain - as well as what I've done to hurt them. These things no longer sit at the forefront of my mind because I've processed them, laid them at the feet of Jesus and I've forgiven. But I cannot forget.

Forgiving then forgetting isn't just impossible, it's also dangerous. We need to remember the lessons that come with the process of forgiving and the realities of what has happened in our lives. I contend that if we forget then there's no point in forgiveness. So the whole "forgive and forget" notion is not viable. It's an assumption being drawn from our human rationale and a seed planted by the enemy to take us on a never-ending journey to forget, that will eventually cause us great harm.

The Bible says in **Psalm 103:12** that Jesus forgives us our sins and that **He will cast our sins as far as the east is to the west,** remembering them no more. Jesus will. We are not Jesus. We are told to forgive. Whatever He asks of us, He will give us the strength, ability, and insight to do. Including forgive others. The reality is in order to forgive we usually have to put in a bit more effort than we think we do or than we feel we have the strength to do.

Hebrews 8:12 also says, **"And I will forgive their wickedness, and I will never again remember their sins."** Yes, we are to be Christ-like. As Christians we're supposed to follow in

Jesus' footsteps, seeking wisdom and counsel in the decisions we make. Forgiving is Christ-like. We were made to be able to forgive and commanded to do so. We were not commanded to forget. The Bible says that He remembers their sins no more. We have to remind ourselves that we are not Jesus and pretending that we can actually forget something is again a human worldly expectation. Perhaps it's more of a wish on our part? Wouldn't it be easier than doing the work to forgive; easier than going through the emotions, the hurt and pain, and the need to lean on the Lord to help us through it?

Remembering the lessons

The fact is, in any circumstance where I needed to forgive someone else, had I actually forgotten the entire incident, and then I would never have learned the lessons I did. In simple terms, if I had forgotten the whole incident when I broke my leg, I wouldn't have learned how to navigate more safely in the snow. I wouldn't remember to dress appropriately so I don't get hypothermia and I wouldn't be able to remember to wear the right footwear. I would then likely make the same mistakes again. Forgetting would just set me up to possibly break my leg again. Forgetting would cause me to forget the lessons I learned and the blessings that eventually came out of that experience. While I was the one I had to forgive in that incident, it was forgiveness all the same. This also goes for serious, hurtful situations and occurrences in our lives. If we truly were able to choose to forget, and we did, what lessons would we retain? What truths would we have lost in the process of forgetting? And how would we ever have been able to grow from it?

When I believed the lie that we had to forgive and forget, I would forgive and then I would work hard to try to forget, or at least pretend that I could forget. I'd push it all to the back of my mind. Then I'd let the same person back in my life to hurt me all over again. Then I would forgive, and then I'd forget, and then they'd do it all again. On and on it went because I allowed the whole process to start over… again and again and again. Sound familiar? Perhaps you can relate. That pattern of trying to "forgive and forget" was the weakness I used to have. That's where we have to beware. We have to realize that this kind of pattern of forgiving and attempting to forget is not of God. It's rooted in a lie we've believed and in the dangerous idea that we can accomplish something that only Jesus can. It's the thing that made me seem like a pushover. My forgiving nature allowed me to walk in obedience. My attempting to forget and in the process allowing the same things to happen to me over and over again was my weakness. This bad pattern set me up for continual, repetitive hurts, manipulation, and a pattern of being used by other people.

When I was going to school for my Master's degree, I was overwhelmed with the process of learning. But I was also elated with it. I loved to talk about what I was learning, especially what I was learning about parts of the Bible I hadn't read before. I would frequently have in-depth Biblical talks with someone we went to church with. He became a friend to my family and we eventually considered him a part of our family. Over time our discussions about the Bible became bizarre. His stance on some things became argumentative. His behavior was erratic. His ability to manipulate me was frightening. If he felt hurt from anything going on in his life he would take it out on me. He was unable to keep a job. We helped him get a car, an apartment, and more than one new job. He never kept them for very long. It took us far too long to realize that he had some severe mental health and spiritual issues that we couldn't help him with. After numerous verbal attacks and a serious assault on my husband, he eventually moved away and we completely disconnected from him. We found out a few years later that he had since been incarcerated.

It took me a long time to overcome the pain of the ups and downs of that relationship and the guilt I felt for not seeing more clearly who he was and what his problems were from the beginning.

I felt guilty for not being able to help him and for allowing my family to become close to him. But if I had simply been able to forgive and forget, I wouldn't have learned the lessons I needed to learn about identifying signs of mental health issues. If I had simply forgotten that whole experience, I would have missed out on the blessings that came out of it. Before the serious incidents that came out of that time period, my husband and I had been extremely stressed, having issues with our son and we became emotionally disconnected. I felt as if I couldn't rely or lean on my husband. We took everything out on each other. After all the turmoil we faced and how we felt threatened by this person we thought was a friend and a family member, I expected things to get worse between my husband and me. But instead, my husband stepped up in ways he never had before. He and I learned so much as we grew together.

Our eyes were opened during that difficult time. We saw each other, our marriage, and our relationship with God in a new light. It was like we had been living in a dark tunnel just staring at the light at the end instead of truly walking in the light. Seeing how hurt and scared I was, my husband was there for me. He hadn't been in a very long time. We allowed the Lord to be the light in the darkness that He is rather than trying to see our way through on our own. Had my husband and I simply been able to forget all about what happened during that painful time, rather than simply forgiving that person and each other, we wouldn't still remember the truths we found out about God, ourselves, or each other. I wouldn't have known that my husband would actually be there for me to lean on. God used this circumstance to begin to heal our marriage after a tumultuous time that had culminated in the idea that we surely would never make it. We did make it. We're still making it today. But only because of our faith in Jesus Christ, the way He has grown us, and the lessons we've learned. I will always be thankful for the lessons remembered, that were born out of the obedience to forgive.

Think about how much more pain, heartache, and trouble we would all get into if we forgot the lessons that come with the pain we went through and the forgiveness we had to give. How many relationships and bad situations would we continually find ourselves in – over and over and over again – because we forgot after we forgave? We would open ourselves up to being hurt the same way again and again because not only did we initially work to forgive but we forgot what in the world we forgave; how it happened, and how we got in that mess in the first place.

The whole "forgive and forget" philosophy leans heavily on the premise that if you're able to put the wrongdoing out of your mind then that's the same as or as good as forgiving. If we simply forget the sin then we won't hold it against someone. But that's not the same thing as forgiveness. Remember, forgiving is defined as ceasing to feel anger toward someone or something and to pardon. Can you do that if you forget? No. You cannot pardon someone if you forget what you're pardoning them for. If you pretend there is nothing to pardon, that's not the same as offering forgiveness.

Releasing the grip of unforgiveness is about ceasing resentment and anger. Ceasing literally means to gradually come to an end.** We cannot choose to cease if we've forgotten, or are unable to recall something. It's simply just not the same as forgiving. Pardoning means the excusing of an offense without exacting a penalty. Just as Jesus did for us. He forgave without exacting a penalty against us. Those things are not the same as forgetting. Had we been told to forget, there would be no need to forgive. **

Even when you know without a shadow of a doubt that you've forgiven someone or yourself, that doesn't mean you'll forget. And I say thank God for that reality. Time and forgiveness will often soften the memory of whatever we need to forgive but they won't necessarily let us totally forget. In the remembering though, after we've forgiven, we are able to learn, to grow and if the forgiveness is for ourselves then we are able to truly repent from the depth of our soul, enabling us to turn away from our sins.

The world wants you to forget about God

Probably the worst consequence there could ever be from simply being able to forget and even in pretending to forget, is that we would forget whatever it was God got us through and that He is the reason we came out the other side in the first place. We would forget the lessons we learned, and worse yet, we would forget what it feels like for His hand of strength to support us. If I simply forgot when I should have forgiven during that dark time with my husband and me, then I would have forgotten that I could actually count on him. I would also forget that I can lean on Jesus. I would have forgotten the many big and small ways the Holy Spirit comforted us, enlightened us, and gave us knowledge we never had before and how good and faithful He is to us.

In forgetting, we would also lose the memory of His loving presence surrounding us in the middle of our devastation, our heartache, our loss, our heartbreak, our victimization; whatever IT is that we had to forgive and were falsely led to believe we could simply forget. I don't know about you but I never want to get so caught up in my own anger, pain, purposeful pretending, or self-righteousness that I forget what God's grace is.

That I could choose to forget how He helped me stand up under what I just went through is a frightening thought to me. I don't want to ever forget that He's got me or that there are streams in the desert and He can take dry bones and make them alive! I think our little amazing, precious human brains would easily erase the truth that there's something called grace that we not only receive, unworthy as we are, but that we are also supposed to give. And again, if we simply forgot then would we ever really have to go through the process of forgiving? There would never have been any need for the many times in the Bible where it tells us to forgive, like in **Luke 6:37** where it says **"Do not judge, and you will not be judged. Do not condemn, and you will not be condemned. Forgive, and you will be forgiven"**

My encouragement to you is to forget about forgetting. Let go of the worldly saying that we're to "forgive and forget" and focus your energy, your prayers, and your love towards forgiving. Remember that forgiving others is a commandment, not a suggestion. Obedience is always easier than disobedience and the painful regret that comes from it. Not only does forgiving others put us in the category of being obedient followers of Jesus Christ, but it also sets us up to be forgiven. **Matthew 6:14** tells us, **"If you forgive those who sin against you, your**

heavenly Father will forgive you."

The world wants us to forget the transgressions. Satan wants us to buy into the whole "forgive and forget" mantra because if we forget the transgression, then we also end up forgetting God's grace and strength in the middle of it. If we forget, then we no longer need to lean on His strength or stand on the truth in the Word of God. That's a scary proposition that's been made to us. Choose the path of least resistance in the moment but then leave God out. The enemy wants you to push the actions and hurt inside to a place where you can pretend to forget so it will come out later as a destructive force against you. And when you do so, the enemy also succeeds in getting you to forget about God and His commandment to forgive.

Forgiveness can be a painful process but we must remember that we're called to do it. That which He calls us to do, He will equip us to do. That which we don't have the strength to do, He will give us the strength to do. **Isaiah 40:29 says He gives strength to the weary and increases the power of the weak.** Learn to lean on the truths in His Word as He reminds us that He is our strength. **Joshua 1:9 tells us Have I not commanded you? Be strong and courageous. Do not be afraid; do not be discouraged, for the LORD your God will be with you wherever**

you go."

Something that also helps me when I think about forgiving others, who in my human estimation don't deserve it, is to remember that forgiving them is not condoning what they do. It is not agreeing with how they dealt with things. It's not an eternal forgiveness either. It's an earthly, human forgiveness. Only God can deal with their true eternal forgiveness, justice, and judgment. Mine is only to forgive and to restore a relationship if it's called for or to forgive and let them go. Again, we have to embrace the truth that forgiveness is ceasing to hold resentment and anger as well as pardoning them. We are not the ones who will exact the judgment or punishment. God will take care of that in His timing and His way.

What it comes down to

If we didn't have some memory of what we forgave or what we were forgiven for, we'd keep making the same mistakes over and over again. Think about it this way, if we didn't remember the pain we got from putting our hand on a hot burner, we'd just put it right back on it and get burned again, right?

Jesus is the one who said that He would cast our sins as far as the East is from the West, remembering them no more. The Bible says we are to forgive others but it doesn't say forget. If we forgot the hurt, the sin, the pain someone else inflicted on us or that we sadly inflicted on another, then we'd have little or no need to forgive, would we? We'd just forget and move on. We wouldn't feel compelled to forgive or to change and grow within ourselves. We wouldn't have any sense of conviction or correction either. And in the forgetting, we would also forget that WE have been forgiven by Jesus. We would forget that somewhere in our sin or in our pain, He was there for us. He brought us through it. Not only did he set us free – He carried us through. Would you want to forget that you're called to love, honor, worship, and glorify Jesus? I wouldn't.

I've met so many people at conferences and retreats who have come up to me later and said that such a burden has been lifted from them just in the knowing that they don't have to forget. The daily work they were trying to do to forget had become such a chore like an albatross around their neck pulling them down. They were so heavily burdened by the guilt they felt because they simply couldn't forget, no matter how hard they tried, that it interfered with all their relationships and distanced them from God. They thought something was wrong with them because they couldn't forget when all the while what they needed to do was be obedient in their forgiving. So let's not enable Satan to convince us of something that will create a chasm between us and our Father. Let's not give the world room in our heads by believing and repeating the lie that we must "forgive and forget". Let's all agree going forward that we will forget about the forgetting and focus on the forgiving.

Woman of God, Let Go:

- If you have engrained in your mind that you must "forgive and forget" then I encourage you to read these scriptures that talk about the Lord's grace and mercy. See for yourself what true grace looks like.
  o Psalm 103:10-13
  o Matthew 18:23-35
  o Luke 7:41-50
  o Matthew 18:21-35
- Do you have things you've forgiven others for and yet they keep coming up at you? Do you have consistent reminders of those events? My question is, have you truly forgiven or did you merely attempt to forget the pain, hoping that in forgetting, the forgiving would also be done? Take the time to talk about those things with the Lord. Ask Him to shine a light on your heart and mind so you can identify if you've actually forgiven them or if you've

just pretended to forget, hoping that effort alone would be enough.

- Are you caught in a cycle of saying you forgave, trying to forget, and then allowing the same thing to happen over and over again? Are you stuck in a pattern of letting someone hurt you and are unsure of how to get off that roller coaster? Repeat to yourself daily that forgetting is not the same as forgiving. Write down the scriptures in the Bible about what forgiveness and grace are and work to memorize them or keep them handy. When you're tempted to just push a memory out of your head of someone you haven't forgiven, take it straight to the Lord and remind yourself that your goal is to forgive and be obedient in doing so.

*If you have bad dreams, memories that haunt you, anger you can't seem to get rid of, and serious side effects from these, such as drug or alcohol use, binging, purging, self-harm, abuse, explosive anger, and thoughts of suicide or homicide, please seek professional help and assistance as you may have PTSD from your experiences. This book is not intended to take the place of any type of mental health, emotional, or ministerial counseling. Just know that in your process,

God's got you, and though I may not know you, God does, and you are being prayed for.

**As defined by Miriam Webster.

KAREN MCCRACKEN

FORGIVENESS IS HEALTHIER THAN UNFORGIVENESS

I'll forever be thankful that I learned from the Bible and personal experience that I need to forgive. It's not merely a suggestion, it's an imperative. **Ephesians 4:32** says that we should **"be tenderhearted to each other and forgive each other just as Christ has forgiven us"**. We should not take that lightly, however, because of my forgiving nature, I have been told more times than I can count that I'm too forgiving. Have you ever been told that? I have news for you. I've learned what I suspected for a long time is true - you cannot be too forgiving. It does not make you weak to forgive. It makes you stronger; healthier even.

The National Library of Medicine's PubMed webpage cites a medical research paper from February 2022 as follows: "Empirical studies have shown that forgiveness decreases anger, anxiety, and depression and increases self-esteem and hopefulness for the future. However, research on the relationship between various outcomes of forgiveness is scarce." *

In other words, studies show that physiologically and psychologically, forgiving others has a positive effect on your health, although various long-term outcomes such as what it does to your levels of anger, depression, and anxiety over time have to be further tracked and researched. I'm not a researcher but I'd be willing to go out on a limb and say from my own experience that the incidents of each of these mental and emotional issues go down in people who have forgiven major hurts and trauma in their life and more so for those who learn to forgive frequently, not allowing unforgiveness to create a stronghold or a place for the devil to attack them repeatedly.

Can you even imagine for a moment what the world would be like if we forgave easily? If we were on the ready with a Christ-like grace and compassion for those around us? In my mind, whether fully rational or not, the very act of such expansive, consistent forgiveness would create a world with less war, more peace, and perhaps substantially better mental health. Better mental health can also be connected to better physical health. Webmd.com states: "Although the mind and body are often viewed as separate, mental and physical health are closely related. Good mental health can positively affect your physical health. In return, poor mental health can negatively affect your physical health."

When we talk about health we can't ignore the most

important health, which is spiritual. Spiritual health affects us mentally and physically. Obedience is a sign of being spiritually healthy. Even the desire to be obedient puts us in a different category than straight-up disobedience does. When we tend to the needs of our soul by being diligent in our prayer life, worship, Bible study, meditation, and our quest to be obedient to what the Word says and what God leads us to do in our lifetime, we're setting ourselves up to feel better inside and out. I believe that when we face difficult physical challenges and health problems, making sure we are in alignment spiritually with the Word and doing what the Lord calls us to do can only help during those challenging times.

I met a woman at a conference in Arizona in 2007. She was an angry person. The topic I went to speak about was Running On E'. It's a whole conference experience I do where the main thread throughout each session is about making sure we don't run on empty. So many people, especially women, run around taking care of everyone else, staying busy, putting too much on their plates, and then they have nothing left for God or for themselves. They go and go and go till they run out of fuel and instead of taking the time to fuel up with life-sustaining, eternal fuels, they go for a quick-fix, dirty fuel like binge-watching TV shows, and immersing themselves in social media. They fuel up with food, shopping, sex, social media attention, and sometimes with more destructive fixes such as drugs, alcohol and porn. When stressed we tend to fuel up in the moment on whatever we have access to that's quick and easy. If it will make us feel good, perk us up, or give us a high for a short period, we do it. If it seems as if it will make us feel less stressed, depressed, or anxious in the moment, it's easier to justify filling up on it. When we're worn out, we tend to go for those quick fixes instead of reaching for what truly sustains us through the Word, prayer, and worship.

After speaking at the main session of this conference about this topic, a woman sought me out. She found me in the ladies restroom. There was a couch and chair there in a little side sitting area. We sat and talked. She cried and poured her heart out to me. She'd recently been recovering from a severe panic attack that took its toll on her. Previous to that she had been in a car accident. Thankfully it was a solo accident where she had veered off the road and hit a tree. She hadn't slept well or much in 3 years and she often found herself sleepy at the wheel. She broke her right foot in the accident when she tried to slam on the brakes. Besides these issues, her hair was falling out, she couldn't keep weight on, she never felt like eating and she was having major anxiety attacks.

This sweet woman shared with me that all her stress started three years earlier when she discovered her husband of twenty-five years was having an affair with a woman at church. In the ongoing divorce proceedings, she later found out that he also had numerous other affairs over the years that she hadn't known about. She was devastated. Though she had gone to counseling and eventually worked through her anger and the sudden changes to her finances, marital status, and her eventual move to a different church, she harbored unforgiveness and resentment toward him. Her therapist told her that her inability to forgive was killing her. She didn't believe it. She went to her doctor and had a myriad of tests to find out what was wrong and nothing came up. As she poured her heart out to me she shared that in the middle of the conference, she realized that her therapist and doctor were correct. Her issue was her inability to forgive. It was killing her. Running away from obedience and clinging to her unforgiveness had taken a huge toll on her life. She had been fueling herself up with anger, resentment, quick fix filthy fuels like over-taking prescription meds, too much caffeine, and binging on TV and movies so that she didn't have to deal with her pain. We prayed together for the Lord to show her how to forgive.

This woman, and so many other women's stories, along with my own experiences, are partly what prompted me to write this book. The downturn in my own health every single time I have held on to unforgiveness has been stark. Witnessing this woman's health and hearing her story, along with other's stories throughout my speaking journey have made the truth all too real. Not only should we be obedient to what it says in **Ephesians 4:32**, but we don't have time to be anything but obedient to it. Our mental, emotional, and spiritual health depends upon it. And yes, our physical health depends upon it as well.

Woman of God, Let Go:

- Have you observed unforgiveness affecting your health in any way? Take some time to think and pray about it. Make a list of ways that unforgiveness may have affected your mental, emotional, spiritual, and physical health.

> Note: This book is not a substitute for seeing a doctor if you need attention for a health issue. The grip of unforgiveness may well have a serious effect on your health but if you have signs and symptoms of health issues, please take the time to go to your doctor and seek his or her expert advice to rule out any other issues.

- Is there a particular thing, action, or person you have not forgiven that is affecting your health? Document it. This is something you'll want to address so you can become fully obedient to Jesus' call to forgive.

* The National Library of Medicine's Pubmed webpage site a medical research paper, health page PMC10120569

FORGIVING SELF

I would be remiss if I didn't address what is likely for many people the most difficult form of forgiveness to offer up and that's self-forgiveness. Oftentimes, even when we become consistent, heart-felt forgivers who have released the grip of unforgiveness of others on our lives, we've still not done the work it takes to forgive ourselves. Again, modern culture, worldly ideas, and the overt lies of Satan tend to make up our mindset and belief about self-forgiveness. What do the examples in the world tell us about forgiving ourselves? Similar to forgiving others, the world tells us that there is no need for forgiving ourselves. We're given the mantras from the world that everything is okay, live and let live, we're all human, we all mess up, just put it out of our minds, there is no need for sorry. Again, we're told to forget about it and move forward.

The world also tells us that certain people with

high-level income and social status don't have to grow, change, or embrace self-forgiveness or forgiveness in any form. Yet, **1 John 1:9 says "If we confess our sins, he is faithful and just and will forgive us our sins and purify us from all unrighteousness."** Seeing someone walk in that forgiveness and be purified is an amazing sight. It's definable, noticeable, admirable, and a witness like no other.

If you have a certain amount of money, you can seemingly live as you please, leaving a trail of sin and destruction in your wake in today's world. Just look around at society. Even when a highly public figure does something that's overtly wrong, like stealing, having an affair, doing drugs, or possessing illegal weapons, there is little to no talk about the need for repentance or for those people to make things right. There doesn't seem to be many examples showing that these highly public figures think they need to give or seek forgiveness. After all, seeking forgiveness from the Lord first and foremost comes from a place of humbleness, confession, and repentance. Do I know the mindset and personal relationship that so many of these public figures have with the Lord? No, none of us can truly know that. But I can see some of the fruit they bear. We can also see the outward expression and result of repentance if it's present.

It doesn't take much to research poor deeds,

criminal charges, and public displays of transgressions that can be attributed to celebrities and public figures. You can view their actions and hear gossip about them pretty much anywhere you look. I do my best to avoid that kind of news but it's everywhere. I think to myself how thankful I am that I haven't put myself in a position to be judged by millions of people for something I said or did. While I feel for people in those positions having their lives on display, at the same time, each of these public figures also has the responsibility to set an example. Perhaps their goal was never to do so but their agreement to become known internationally or nationally comes with the inherent disclaimer that their lives will very much be on public display in some form or fashion. Everyday citizens, children of God, celebrity status, or online social media stars alike will all have to answer for their actions and how they have influenced others. That's the reality. Whether we agree with what any of these famous people do or don't do, we have a responsibility to look out for the generations to come. One of the ways we can do that is by setting an example of Godliness, love, compassion, forgiveness, and truth in the way we live and in the fruit we bear. That includes whether or not we are forgivers of others and ourselves.

What does repentance have to do with self-forgiveness?

Signs that someone is repentant of something they've done wrong don't come in the form of some showy outward declaration shouted from the rooftops or in some public confession posted online. According to The Gospel Coalition, "Repentance is defined as a heartfelt conviction of sin, a contrition over the offense to God, a turning away from the sinful way of life, and a turning towards a God-honoring way of life. Any or all of these may apply to various transgressions."

The number of popular celebrities, social media influencers, famous sports figures, and politicians who are paraded in the public venue, proud of their sins and happy to influence others is growing every day. Knowing that what they say or do will be sadly emulated and seen as acceptable, speaks of the perverse nature of digital culture and rampant social media influences. It's a rare occasion to see a celebrity take to their public outlets to express regret in a humble manner and then see their repentant actions in the days and years after, although it does occasionally happen. The fact is, whether it's a celebrity or someone you know personally if they've sought forgiveness from the Lord, one key component of it is repenting. Repenting includes turning away from the sinful actions and turning towards God. If that isn't happening then true repentance hasn't happened.

Repentance doesn't mean that someone is instantly incapable of repeating that sin or is then miraculously the person you hope them to be. Can that happen? Yes. God can convict and change anyone in an instant. (Remember Paul on the road to Damascus? **Read Acts 9:1-9**.) So, yes, God can do anything with a person who is moved, convicted, and willing. But in most cases, it takes time to process, repent, and take on the responsibility to change. The fact is, with repentance comes the willingness and even eagerness to make those changes and turn away from the transgression, in order to move closer to God. **Romans 8:1-2** tells us **"So now there is no condemnation for those who belong to Christ Jesus. And because you belong to him, the power of the life-giving Spirit has freed you from the power of sin that leads to death."** In the type of display where repentance has clearly happened, condemnation has been left behind, and the power of the Spirit shines through is a mighty example to anyone who is blessed to see it manifest in the life of someone else.

I share all this about repentance to say that without repentance, self-forgiveness isn't possible. Unless we acknowledge that we've sinned and taken responsibility for it in some form or fashion, we won't understand the depth to which our actions have affected our mindset and decisions. Without repenting of our sins, we can't fully embrace the reasons we need forgiveness from Jesus or from ourselves. It's not about publicly confessing. It's about having a deeper relationship with Jesus Christ. It's not about apologizing or making amends, although in some cases that might apply. Forgiving yourself is a personal process and just like unforgiveness of others that you've held on to, not forgiving yourself can have dire consequences in your daily life.

The signs that you haven't forgiven yourself are similar to those that occur when you have held on to unforgiveness of others.

3 signs you haven't forgiven yourself

Sign #1 - When you try to rest, your mind takes you to that person, that thing, or that action that you haven't forgotten, because most likely you can't forget it – but if it's consistently coming to mind, causing you to spiral down emotionally and mentally, then you're holding on to guilt, fueled by unforgiveness of yourself.

Sign # 2 – You haven't let go of the anger you feel towards yourself or about that situation. You may find yourself feeling angry one moment and justifying your actions the next. You bounce back and forth between guilt, anger, and defense. Remember the definition of forgiveness is "Ceasing to resent, to stop feeling anger. To pardon." When you pardon yourself, you release yourself from exacting a punishment. Are you punishing yourself for things you haven't sought the Lord's forgiveness for and consequently you're still holding on to unforgiveness towards yourself?

Sign #3 – You're making insults, negative and derogatory comments about yourself. Do you find yourself saying negative things about yourself or calling yourself things like stupid, idiot, or unloved? The names can get worse than that when you've let unforgiveness take over and plant seeds of unworthiness. When you believe the lie that Satan wants us all to believe – the one that says none of us is worthy of love and none of us can be forgiven – then you have opened the door to self-deprecating thoughts and words. If you find yourself constantly down on who you are and yet what you've done of late is fantastic, then you haven't forgiven yourself of some past transgression.

Sign #4 – You withdraw from church, loved ones, and normal activities you used to enjoy. When we haven't forgiven ourselves for something, be it a small thing or a big thing, we tend to push away those we love. We retreat into hiding out of embarrassment and sometimes it's because we don't want to see disappointment or hurt in the eyes of those we care about. Withholding forgiveness of yourself can have dire consequences just like withholding forgiveness of others can. It can separate families, create unstable mental health situations, and cause depression, anxiety, and loss of desire to work or care for ourselves.

Letting the grip of unforgiveness keep us from forgiving ourselves for past sins and current transgressions is like drinking poison as a form of punishment. For those of us who love Jesus and want to live an obedient life, we tend to hold on to self-punishment instead of embracing self-forgiveness. It's so easy to become judge, jury, and executioner of our own story.

Psalm 32:5 says: **"Finally, I confessed all my sins to you and stopped trying to hide my guilt. I said to myself, "I will confess my rebellion to the LORD." And you forgave me! All my guilt is gone."**

Peter's example

When I was studying about forgiveness and I read the verses about Peter, knowing that Peter was asking Jesus about how many times he should forgive others, I realized that perhaps Peter had himself in mind when he asked that question. How many times do you see Peter throughout Scripture act impulsively and make decisions out of fear? Decisions he later regretted? He cut off the ear of one of the soldiers who tried to arrest Jesus and was admonished by Jesus for doing so.

(**John 18:10-11**) Peter is one of those figures in the Bible we could all relate to, I'm sure. He fails miserably at many things. At one point when Jesus calls him out on the water, Peter rises and is astonished to walk on the water. First, he doubts but then he steps out and does it but only to then fear the wind, taking his eyes off Jesus and falling because of it. (**Matthew 14:22**) Isn't that how most of us are? We keep our eyes on Jesus until fear hits us, and then we look elsewhere for the answers but we end up falling. We fail.

In **Matthew 18:21-35** when Peter asks Jesus about how many times he should forgive, I realize now that Peter wasn't just asking for the world at large or because there were people he didn't want to have to forgive. He was likely asking because he knew how much he needed forgiveness. In that conversation and in later actions of his, we can clearly see that Peter lived a life fraught with guilt. Peter's guilt and shame from denying Jesus three times, (**Matthew 26:31-35**) even after Jesus confronted him, became evident when Peter died. History records that when Peter was martyred for telling people about Jesus Christ he refused to be hung on the cross in the manner Jesus was. He requested he be hung upside down. He felt he wasn't worthy to die in the manner Jesus died.*

"One of the greatest lessons that Peter teaches us is how to deal with past sin, especially if it's something big, nasty, and outright embarrassing.

The devil's great trick is to make us think that God couldn't possibly forgive certain sins, because they're just too severe. Even if we've confessed certain sins, and in our heads we know that God is merciful and has forgiven us, sometimes just thinking back to those embarrassing moments makes us doubt the power of God's mercy and the fact that He truly can make all things new. But Peter's story reminds us that those kinds of thoughts are from the Evil One. God is not a liar and He truly does make all things new for those who accept His merciful love."

"When Peter looked back and thought about that time he denied Jesus, or the time he couldn't walk on water, or the time Jesus told him, "Get behind me, Satan." *He looked back on those sins not as sins committed but as sins confessed and forgiven.* When we sin, we need to admit it and ask the Lord's forgiveness." - Father Damien Ference **

When we do as it says here in this quote by Father Damien Ference and look on our sins not as something we have committed but as something we have confessed and been forgiven of, it's then that we can process what we've done, remove the guilt and be open to conviction on how we change course. Once we accept that we have to change course and we have to repent and turn away from those sins, that's when our guilt, shame, and unforgiveness of self stops having a grip on our lives.

Woman of God, Let Go:

- Do you have a list in your head of things you're holding against yourself? Sins and wrong-doings you think are unforgivable? They are not unforgivable. Go to the Lord with that list. Old sins, new sins, all sins. Take them to the Lord and ask Him to shine the light on them so you can deal with them. Seek His forgiveness and strength to repent.

- To make amends or not make amends? When it comes to making amends we have to be cautious. Often our desire to make amends with someone comes out of a desire to rid ourselves of guilt. The rule of thumb here is the same as the rule of thumb for people going through a 12-step recovery program. Lesson 16 in the Celebrate Recovery step program is about making Amends. Their rule of thumb is: "Evaluate all my relationships. Offer forgiveness to those who have hurt me and make amends for harm I've done to others, <u>except when to do so would harm them or others</u>"

  If your goal in making amends, apologizing, or offering some sort of restitution is to ease your own guilt, don't do it. Let Jesus guide you. Be open to the Holy Spirit's prompting in this and be without doubt before you proceed. If reaching out to someone will cause harm and undue stress to them or someone they love, then it's not the course of action you should take. If that's the case then let it go and focus on simply being obedient to God rather than attempting to make amends.

- Offering forgiveness to others, confessing your sins, and seeking forgiveness from God is the first step in the process of stopping your own guilt and self-punishment. When you're able to do these things, it frees you to forgive yourself as well. To become free from the grip of unforgiveness though, we have to remember that pouring out those transgressions to God and embracing the freedom that comes from repentance is necessary for you to release that grip of unforgiveness you hold over yourself. Now is the time to let go and start your journey to release the grip that unforgiveness of yourself may hold on you.

*https://seanmcdowell.org/blog/was-peter-crucified-upside-down

**Wordonfire.com

THE CYCLE OF UNFORGIVENESS

Robert Assagioli said, "Without forgiveness, a human's life is governed by an endless cycle of resentment and retaliation."

Oh, did that strike you at your core? For some it does. It hits close to home for those who have been harboring resentment for years and never dealt with forgiving others. Forgiveness isn't a trade or a tool we learn to utilize in school or Voc Ed classes. Even in Christian environments, though many were taught morals, as well as the Ten Commandments, memorizing scripture, and who the main Bible characters were, most of us were not taught about forgiveness and why it's so important for us to give it. We'll know about the forgiveness of Jesus Christ given to us but to be able to claim forgiveness as something we readily know how to give, is not that common. Most of us know that we're supposed to give it and that's about it.

Perhaps you're one of those who has never learned how to forgive or understood how freeing it is to let go of the unforgiveness you've learned to hold on to. Again, most of us weren't taught from a young age what forgiveness is. Instead, we were taught to just "let it go", which usually meant not ever bringing it up again; never addressing the situation, and pretending everything was fine just so we could keep the peace in the moment. Sadly, that type of teaching leads directly to what Rover Assagioli cautioned us about resentment and retaliation.

We weren't taught why forgiveness of others or even of self is so important or what's Biblical about it or how freeing it is to give it. Assagioli's quote states that forgiveness keeps us from living a life "governed by an endless cycle of resentment and retaliation." That endless cycle can lock us in chains and keep us attached to the very drama and trauma we so want to move beyond in order to live a full, joyful life in the Lord. That's the kind of life I used to live. If you're there, I'm certain you're not alone.

As adults, many of us are just now learning what true forgiveness is all about and praying we muster up the strength and desire to be obedient enough to forgive. Some people, even in the church, don't understand that forgiveness is not supposed to be a rare thing we have to do. We're just learning how much of our mental and emotional health can be affected by a lack of forgiveness and the chain reaction that harboring unforgiveness has on our lives. In the process of becoming aware and frankly finally learning to heed what it says in the Bible about forgiving others, we have to go back to clean up some messes we made in our lives due to holding on to unforgiveness. Today's society is dealing with the residual effects of not forgiving others. In my opinion, these effects have snowballed and propelled so many people into a state of mental illness and weakened spiritual lives that it's created a world where some people, Christians included, are incapable of nurturing healthy relationships, keeping stable jobs, and barely living on a faith that is fading the tighter that grip has hold of us.

When I read that quote about the endless cycle created by not forgiving, it drew me back to scripture. **James 1:5** says, **"If any of you lacks wisdom, let him ask God, who gives generously to all without reproach, and it will be given him."** I am once again in awe of how on target the scriptures are, for without wisdom we cannot forgive. We're told that if we lack it, we should seek God and He will give us that wisdom without reproach. In some ways, many of us would have preferred God to simply spell out directions in a bit more concrete, detailed manner but what He has given us is everything we need for this life. It was given with purpose and without reproach. If we would just learn to heed what it says, seek Him when we need guidance, and lean on Him, then our lives would be better, more fulfilling, freer, and healthier. That includes the commandment for us to forgive.

The seemingly endless cycle of resentment and retaliation that Assagoli speaks of can happen because we hold on to one incident or one person that we haven't forgiven or because we perpetually hold on to unforgiveness, not willing to embrace the truth that frequent forgiveness and immediate release of unforgiveness from daily trials and problems is what we're called to do. The disobedient stance of being unwilling to forgive, be it a small grievance or a deep, life-altering event, will cause the endless cycle to begin. That cycle often includes cycles of grief, anger, and self-loathing, eventually ending up in resentment and retaliation. As we're encouraged by the enemy to embrace unforgiveness instead of obedience to God's Word on the subject of forgiving others, we set up a place where unforgiveness has a hold on us: a tight, mental, emotional, and spiritual grip on our daily walk, our relationships with others and on our view of the world. It can easily lead us down a path of destruction.

Take heart though, because even though holding on to unforgiveness and the side effects of it may seem like an endless cycle, with the Lord's help we can put an end to it.

The quest to end the cycle

While I've barely scratched the surface of unforgiveness, rest assured that the details, stories, how-to's, and encouragement to help you end the unhealthy cycle of unforgiveness within these pages were meant for not just me but for you as well. Through Biblical perspectives, scripture, wise words from fellow Christians, and testimonies from others who have been in the grip of unforgiveness and who were able to finally let go, my prayer is that you will soon be on your way to releasing the grip of unforgiveness as well.

Woman of God, Let Go:

- Go now before the throne of God and seek Him to show you through His eyes if you have any past or present unforgiveness gripping you. Practically speaking, sit with a notepad and pen or get your Notes App opened up on your phone so you can write down what He shows you as you pray for guidance.
- Write down the insights, situations, events, and people God places on your heart as you pray for Him to show you where you

haven't truly forgiven and where unforgiveness still has a grip on you.

- Now pray for God to illuminate any chain reaction that has happened in your life because of your unforgiveness. Are there bad choices you've made, relationships you've severed, people you've lashed out at, or purposefully hurt because you ended up in a cycle of resentment and retaliation? Write these down and ask Him to strengthen you through this process. (We'll come back to this list again in later chapters so tuck it in a notebook or file it away but continue to pray in your quiet time for His revelation in this process.)

A DAILY ATTITUDE OF FORGIVENESS

One of my favorite quotes is from the famous American author and motivational speaker, Zig Ziglar. He wrote a book called Confessions of a Happy Christian as well as numerous other best-selling books. He consistently spoke about his faith in God and living a life with depth and meaning. About forgiveness, he said, "In the blink of an eye, everything can change. So forgive often and love with all your heart. You may never have the chance again."

Here's the catch in this brilliant quote from Mr. Ziglar: in order to forgive often, we have to realize that there will frequently be things to forgive. Going through life with our heads in the sand, thinking that drama, trauma, and pain will only be an occasional thing is not realistic. It's just not true. All these things happen to most human beings at one time or another, including to Christians. We aren't immune to the traumas of life or tragedy. It's part of reality. But we can't run from reality. Sooner or later it will catch up to us and when we don't prepare ourselves to forgive the eventual forthcoming pain of drama and trauma, we're not only being disobedient to God's Word, we're also setting ourselves up for prolonged pain because we believe we can somehow avoid the unforgiveness we're holding tightly to by ignoring it.

Unforgiveness, no matter who is harboring it, festers. It becomes an infected injury in our minds and our emotions. It eventually causes us to become spiritually stagnant. Making a practice of forgiving often and without bias is essential to healthy Christian living and healthy relationships but it's also essential for healthy spiritual growth in our walk with the Lord. So, when Zig Ziglar cautioned us that we should forgive often and love with all our hearts, he knew of what he spoke. In the blink of an eye, everything can indeed change. What and who you're holding on to today could be taken away or lost in a second. When we harbor unforgiveness, we're saying we'd rather hold on to unforgiveness; nursing our hurt, anger, and pride, more than we want to hold on to what matters most in those we love and in Jesus Christ.

Forgiveness in the midst of the storm

I was witness to a display of forgiveness one time when I was traveling that made me see forgiveness not as some grand act we offer up to the occasional person here and there who has wronged us or wounded us but as an act of daily obedience. I'll explain by sharing that experience with you.

We all know there are times that people push us to the point of losing our peace, or at least, creating within us the desire to occasionally throw the whole notion of peace out the window and embrace a little rage. It can take mounds of self-control and tapping into the strength of the Lord to keep ourselves in check. I'm guessing most everyone understands that feeling at one time or another and perhaps, depending on your vocation, you live in that perpetual tug of war.

A few years ago I was flying to Wisconsin and it happened to be on a day when bad storms hit this half of the country. It was horrendous. I heard someone on their cell phone tell what I think was her spouse that there was a "minor delay" in the flight schedule due to the storms. Minor delay?

That's like saying my feet are minor in size! That would be completely inaccurate since I wear a size 11 shoes. I should be 6 feet tall. I'm only 5'6". Somewhere along the family genetic pool, I lost out in that department. The downplaying of the flight delays was a major size 12, triple E delay, not a petite size 6. At that point it had been a 14-hour delay to be exact, followed by another 5-hour delay plus actual flight time. It took 19 hours to get to Minneapolis. I could have driven there and halfway back in that time period. I had to keep looking about and reminding myself to be thankful for what I had so I didn't get sucked into the great vortex of over-the-top, relentlessly rude co-travelers milling around the airport. Many of them let their rage build up quickly and continued to seethe throughout the delay. Some travelers seemed to think that somehow those poor Southwest airline employees could control the weather patterns.

So, here I am in the airport, working to maintain my composure. Exhausted. Aggravated. Disgusted. All the while armoring up so I didn't let the contagious anger other passengers were spewing infect my attitude. I resorted to doing the thing that has always worked for me, and that's to humble myself with thankfulness; glorifying God in the process. There's nothing more eye-opening, simple, and relevant than making yourself aware of your surroundings, both physical and spiritual, to give you a reality check. That reality check is often what I personally need in order to give myself perspective in the moment so I don't go off the deep end mentally or emotionally. So that's what I did. I put myself in a mental state of thankfulness, remembering **Philippians 4:12-13, "I know what it is to be in need, and I know what it is to have plenty. I have learned the secret of being content in any and every situation, whether well-fed or hungry, whether living in plenty or in want. I can do all this through him who gives me strength."**

Looking around the expansive airport, filled with exhausted passengers, I started to thank God for anything and everything I could. After all, even though I felt desperately in need of a comfy bed and some nourishment other than snacks from the convenience store, I had plenty. I knew I needed to focus on being as content as I could be. I talked to God, "Lord, I'm thankful for the footstool I found one gate over and the courage to drag it over here to prop up my injured leg. I'm thankful for the television reporter in front of us in line earlier who made us laugh. I'm thankful I didn't have to crawl under the door in the stall in the ladies' restroom earlier when the door jammed. Thank you for helping me to get out of there. I'm thankful the storms haven't hit here and we still have electricity. I'm thankful I get to fly to Wisconsin for a family wedding. I'm thankful I brought a book with me today and I have a Bible app on my phone. I'm thankful for the safe flight You will eventually bless us with."

Focusing on being thankful took my mind and attitude immediately to a different place. I felt more content. I paid better attention to what was going on around me. I sensed that I was supposed to open my eyes to my surroundings and take it in rather than shut my brain down and sit in a cocoon of self-pity. In doing so, I started to notice the flight personnel coming and going, the attendants at the desk, and the gate and airport staff. I really paid attention. I felt bad for those airline employees. Not just Southwest Airlines but all the airlines. I understood how frustrating it was for us passengers who were stuck. We had no place to go. But neither did the various staff mixed in with us.

I finally ended up wandering around the airport looking at really expensive t-shirts, interesting neck pillows and spending $5 on a pack of gum. But I refused to take my frustrations out on the staff. I determined within my heart and mind to be content in knowing I was being kept safe, even with the aggravating delay. I had more than I needed. I was thankful.

At one point I became hyper-aware of a particular staff at our airline counter. I am quite certain that if this one staff had any choice in the matter, she would have gotten some of the angry travelers out and on a plane ASAP. I giggled to myself thinking that if I were in her shoes I would rebook them on any plane available or perhaps a helicopter or perhaps wrap them in a seat belt, attached to a bungee cord, carried by a drone; just to get them out of my hair. Some of those waiting passengers were utterly unapologetically mean, rude, and confrontational over the whole delay.

As I stood watching how composed this staff stayed throughout it all, I was thinking, "How does she deal with this? How do these flight attendants, pilots, and agents keep these rude, downright insulting people, from getting to them? How do they leave their jobs every day after treatment like this and still want to come back? Just as importantly, how do they not take it out on the passengers, going up one side of them and down the other? What kind of forgiveness of humanity must it take for them to get up and do this every day, knowing they very well may run into a day with another bad storm and angry people? Maybe I'm too sensitive or thin-skinned but I felt like I needed to know what made these people tick. What kept them from coming unglued? Especially that one particular, seemingly unflappable airline agent standing at the desk who I had honed in on.

After about 14 hours of waiting in the airport, they announced that we could get our tickets changed, divert to alternate cities to avoid storms, and be on our way. I lined up, knowing all the while they couldn't guarantee those flights would go out either because all they could do was reissue tickets on different flights and hope the skies in those areas wouldn't soon be storm-filled as well. Within a mere 45 minutes of the announcement, the offer to divert was canceled. The delays wouldn't dissipate as hoped.

I stayed in line at this point to ask a question about whether or not I could be reimbursed if I couldn't get a flight out in time to even make the wedding in Wisconsin. I wasn't relishing the wait time in the line, semi-worrying whether or not I'd find a footstool again for my leg when all the waiting was over. Again, as I was in line, I paid attention to what was right in front of me; a calm, compassionate airline agent. As I gradually made my way up towards the desk I could hear the conversations the passengers in front of me were having with this agent and the words they were hurling at her. All the while, she stayed calm. She spoke smooth as glass; easy peasy. I was sincerely in awe. She had to be as tired, if not more so than I was, yet she maintained a peace and calm I truly admired.

In the semi-defense of some of the highly

frustrated passengers, it wasn't easy to stand for extremely long periods waiting for someone to attempt to help. It was exhausting and frustrating. Weary travelers can easily become agitated. It's not unheard of for someone to lose their cool. But isn't that the challenge for all of us? Not to lose our cool? Not to take out our anger and frustration on others? Other people are not our verbal or physical punching bags. Unfortunately, some people in our line didn't seem to get the memo.

I contemplated this great wonder in front of me though. Whether it was the sugar high from chewing half a pack of gum or just plain awe, I felt like I needed to know what made this woman tick. Why was she so calm in the midst of this literal storm? I felt like I needed to know how and why this ultra-patient airline staff could be so kind and forgiving of the mean-spirited people she was serving. My thoughts landed on the idea that she surely must know how to put a mask on and hide things well, as if she were in a costume, playing a part.

When it was my turn to be assisted I stepped forward, answered her questions, and then waited while she tap, tap, tapped on the keyboard to see if she could find some answers for me. As I was being waited on, a passenger came up to the side of the desk and started yelling at her. He got to the point of being belligerent. She calmly turned to him and said, "Sir, I do understand your frustrations. Unfortunately, there isn't anything I can do to change the situation but if you want to wait in line, I'll see what I can do to make things easier for you once it's your turn." Then she simply turned and continued to assist me. I saw more than one person berate her, cuss, scream, and cry, all the while blaming her for the misfortune of the storm. She had the patience of a saint. I'd overheard another agent talking a few moments before that most of their employees had already been there 6 hours past the end of their shift. As we waited for the computer to spit out the information she needed to assist me, I just asked her, "How can you stay so calm in all this? How do you handle people like that man yelling and cussing at you as if you can control the storms?" She looked at me and said, "Well, I remember they're human and so am I. I breathe and pray through it and every time a new one is rude to me I whisper, "I forgive you". If I don't, then I hold on to it and it stays with me. I don't need that. God is bigger than their rudeness."

How great of an answer is that? She forgives them immediately, speaks it out, turns it over to the Lord, and doesn't hold on to it. "God is bigger than their rudeness." Her answer smacked me right when I needed it. I'd been dealing with some of my own issues with struggling to forgive others I had to deal with on a day-to-day basis and the wisdom she shared through her simple statement made all the difference in the world to me in my quest to forgive. I realized at that moment that I'd allowed all the little daily interactions to be pushed aside, which later built up and bombarded my thoughts, resulting in me holding on to unforgiveness. Those small grains of sand I pretended didn't exist each day became big rocks and sometimes boulders because I refused to deal with them. I was the one who was putting on a mask in the day-in and day-out, rather than being obedient to show compassion and forgiveness. She was right. God is bigger than their anger, their frustration, their sinfulness, their attitude, their cussing, their frustration. God is bigger than our unwillingness to step into someone else's shoes to see life from their perspective. He's bigger than our travel woes, our financial issues, and the worry that builds up when we have them. He is bigger than our sinfulness and bigger than our unforgiving nature. Plain and simple, no matter how big something seems in the moment, God is bigger! I thanked her for her perspective and told her I'd be praying for her. She seemed genuinely touched that I said so.

Remembering that God is bigger than all that chaos served me well throughout the rest of the travel time. I also learned that the airline's sense of humor was bigger than the unruly passenger problem. After 19 hours, when we finally were able to board a flight and it began to take off, the flight attendant was going over the safety procedures and said, "And for those of you who aren't happy with our service here on Southwest or our sense of humor, let me show you where the 8 exits on the plane are. Feel free to use one now."

The forgiveness and sense of humor in a difficult and tense situation inspired me. I've always considered myself a fairly forgiving person, in some sense forgiving others comes naturally to me. Maybe it's a gift or maybe it's because I have two brothers and two sisters and I had no choice since I was the quietest and picked on a whole lot growing up. I mean, I was so quiet that my mom and dad left me sitting in my bouncy chair at home one day when they gathered up the family to go somewhere. Unbeknownst to them they left me there all by myself. They forgot me. It didn't dawn on them till they started asking the rest of the kids in the station wagon, "Where's Karen?" Of course, I didn't need to talk much since I had four other kids doing it for me most days. All I had to do was point, smile, frown, and laugh or cry and someone else would speak up for me. But, as my Dad used to point out, I've successfully more than made up for those days of not talking. And yes, I've forgiven my parents for temporarily abandoning me.

What I walked away from that stormy travel excursion understanding was that forgiveness is not something we put on a shelf and get down on special occasions of intense hurt or betrayal. It's something we're supposed to embrace as part of our everyday walk as Christians. It isn't something set apart only for certain people. Grace is defined as "Unmerited divine assistance given to humans for their regeneration or sanctification." (Miriam Webster). Unmerited means we don't deserve it. We did nothing to earn it. In the Bible, we're told that we're to forgive others. **1 Peter 4: 10-11** tells us that we are to be faithful stewards of God's grace, in all its various forms. We are to be those stewards of grace whether we feel up to it or not.

"Each of you should use whatever gift you have received to serve others, as faithful stewards of God's grace in its various forms. If anyone speaks, they should do so as one who speaks the very words of God. If anyone serves, they should do so with the strength God provides, so that in all things God may be praised through Jesus Christ. To him be the glory and the power forever and ever. Amen." 1 Peter 4:10-11

As stewards of grace and partakers of that same grace and forgiveness, it's our job to show this kind of Christ-like unmerited, unearned grace to others. That's not to say it's easy but in practicing it every single day, during the ups and downs of our daily walk, it gets easier. As the airline agent shared with me, God is bigger than even our own feelings over a situation.

I made it a quest after that trip to work on daily forgiveness. If I was confronted by someone in the grocery store who was rude or belligerent because I parked in the handicapped spot when to them they thought I looked just fine, I prayed through it. I didn't put a fake mask on and pretend it didn't happen, pushing it aside to let it ignite anger in me later. I calmly responded and I spoke to God immediately, asking Him to take it and telling Him I forgave them.

If someone cut me off in traffic and flipped me an unwarranted middle finger, instead of getting hurt or offended, I prayed for them and told God I forgave them. If my husband came home from work in a bad mood because something was bothering him, I would pray for him and myself, in case he decided to snap at me instead of deal with the situation at hand. I'd speak to him calmly and let him know I was sorry that he had a rough day but remind him not to take it out on me. In the past, I would have snapped right back at him and it would take an hour for us both to calm down so we could talk. I learned from the

Southwest airline agent that tackling the mental situation of hurt and offense AS it happens rather than letting it harbor inside us, spreading discontent throughout our being, was the healthiest thing for myself and others. I learned that forgiveness isn't something we always have to take in and ponder, go to the altar with, and pray over. Forgiveness is something that is just supposed to be. In some ways, forgiveness needs to become as easy and simple as breathing in and out. It should be a no-brainer that we are all human and that God says we are to forgive others. It should be a given that grace and forgiveness should be a daily practice.

When everyday forgiveness eludes me, I recall the memory of the airline employee's gracious and forgiving attitude. I reinforce that with the words of Martin Luther King, Jr. "Forgiveness is not an occasional act; it is a permanent attitude."

Woman of God, Let Go:

- Are there everyday hurts, offenses, or misunderstandings you've not forgiven? Are they building, one on top of another and creating a wall between you and someone else in your life? Take time to analyze your closest relationships first. If you're harboring anything against someone else for a minor offense, take it to the

Lord. Determine within yourself, committing to the Lord, that you will forgive and let go of this kind of unforgiveness.

- It may take practice, but on a daily basis start to release offenses soon after they happen. Aggravation, insults, feeling slighted and ignored, teased, or demeaned are all things that happen regularly in today's culture. Be determined to speak out to the Lord. Vent to Him, rather than getting into an argument with someone else. Ask Him to help you do so. Call out the offense and proclaim that you forgive that person/people. Forgiving breaks any power that offense and hurt have over you and takes far less time out of your day than holding on to hurt and anger.

FORGIVING LIKE JESUS

C.S. Lewis said, "To be Christian means to forgive the inexcusable because God has forgiven the inexcusable in you." I agree. While we often hear people say that our quest as followers of Jesus is to be Christ-like, we're usually told that entails things like tithing, attending church regularly, fellowshipping with other Christians, giving to the needy and the poor, serving, and being evangelistic. While all those are good things and some of them are Godly things, none of these is inherently Christ-like.

On the subject of being more like Jesus, writer Chris Sprinkle wrote in a blog in March 2020 "When people say they want to become more like Jesus, they usually mean they want to become a moral person. Such morality is often defined by religious values shaped by a modern Christian subculture, not all of which is bad. My suspicion, though, is that if we look closely at Jesus without our modern moralistic filter, fewer people would want to become more like Jesus." *

The author goes on to talk about how if someone were to truly be more like Jesus and live like He did, that means they would commit to never being married, commit to being celibate, to having the highest sense of morality, and working extremely hard without pay, and to basically work to never, ever mess up. They would commit to having no personal possessions, no wealth, and not even know where their next meal is going to come from. Their moral character would be to the highest level one could imagine if they could manage it. I add though it sounds in jest, that most people wouldn't choose to dress in meager clothing if they had a choice. Most people, contemplating all the Christ-like attributes that modern religion tells us we must take on, need to realize that tithing, modern forms of evangelizing, attending church every time the doors are open and even fellowshipping with other Christians are not things we see Jesus doing in the Bible. These are things spoken of in the Bible by Jesus, Paul, Matthew, and John but are not the historical picture we've been given of how Jesus lived his earthly life. Again, that's not to say these aren't Biblical things, good things, moral things, and things of value. But the fact is, when you think about what is true Christ-like living, most people would not choose to live the way Jesus lived when He was on earth.

The same goes for forgiving someone. Few, if any people, would allow themselves to be put on a cross and crucified in order to forgive others for their sins. Yet, that is exactly what Jesus did for us. We were not called to die on a cross and there's no need. That's already been done for us. No one can take His place. He took our place by being a living sacrifice so that we could be forgiven He pardoned us; and forgave us without exacting a punishment on us for our sins. So, how can we forgive like Jesus and be Christ-like in our actions if we weren't meant to die on a cross? To live and forgive in a Christ-like way is to mimic Jesus' grace, compassion, unmerited favor and forgive without expecting punishment to come upon those we're forgiving. And, to do so with a sincere heart. That type of forgiveness takes a type of strength that doesn't come from being human. First and foremost though it takes us having the sincere desire to be obedient and then it takes us tapping into the strength afforded us by the advocate we have in the Holy Spirit through the love of Jesus.

Just like becoming a Christ-like person doesn't happen in the blink of an eye, most often forgiving others or ourselves doesn't either. It can be something that happens more smoothly, quickly, and with less pain as we become children of God who practice daily and frequent forgiveness, rather than withholding it though. When we resist forgiving, fighting all the way through the process, the grip of unforgiveness feels like it's strangling our faith and our zest for life. It's like a dog on a leash fighting to go in the opposite direction of its master. The dog pulls in one direction when the master wants it to head down a different path. The dog gets choked and ends up hacking and coughing as it tugs and tugs, trying to get its own way. I was that way in the past when it came to being obedient about forgiveness. When I would resist going the way the Master wanted me to, I felt choked and became exhausted with the effort to try to go in the opposite direction of forgiveness. Unforgiveness had a strong hold on me.

When I spoke at a lady's retreat one time, a woman about 70 years old who had quite an attitude toward life, in general, didn't want anything to do with forgiving others. Even though she knew what the Bible said, her opinion was that it was impossible. She said she prayed God would understand when she met Him face to face. She shared with me some deep hurts from her past that she had never forgiven and had no plans of doing so. She said she had led a Christ-like life and she felt good about it. I lightly smiled, reached out, took her hand, and looked her straight in the eye, I asked her why she knew she was saved. She said, "Because Jesus died for me to forgive me of my sins." Then I asked her what she thought was the most important thing Jesus ever did with His life here on earth and she said, "Sacrifice Himself to save others." I smiled and said, "What was Jesus' time spent doing while He was here on earth?" She looked at me like I was ignorant and said, "Well, he spent His time telling everyone about His Heavenly Father and preparing everyone for His death and resurrection."

I looked at her and said, "From what you just told me about Jesus' life, if we want to be Christ-like, the greatest thing we can do is to do the greatest thing He ever did, but as a human being, not as God. So, if He told people about God, His own death and resurrection, then us doing that would be Christ-like?" She agreed. "And then if we are to be Christ-like, shouldn't we also forgive others as He forgave us? Above anything else, wasn't Jesus' entire life about forgiveness?" She just stared at me and started to cry.

Throughout my journey to become more Christ-like in my thoughts and actions, I have learned that the most Christ-like thing I could ever do would be to forgive others. I found out quickly when I spoke about the epidemic of unforgiveness in the church, that many Christians don't have forgiveness on their checklist of what is surely the most Christ-like thing any of us can do. Many I've spoken to even see it as impossible. It's something we are all capable of doing, however. Jesus endured excruciating pain and humiliation to forgive us for our sins. The very least we can do is to endure what we have to endure now to forgive others, even if that takes great emotional or mental pain and effort. We have the advantage and blessing of doing the work it takes by seeking His help in order to be more like Him. We have an advocate, a comforter, and a strong tower to run to when the pain seems like it is more than we can bear. By releasing the grip that unforgiveness has on our lives, it frees us to become more Christ-like. It allows us to release the heavy burden of unforgiveness that weighs us down and to quit playing tug-of-war with our Master.

Part of the process of being obedient to forgive as He calls us to will naturally include being obedient to what it says in **Ephesians 4:31-32, "Get rid of all bitterness, rage and anger, brawling and slander, along with every form of malice. Be kind and compassionate to one another, forgiving each other, just as in Christ God forgave you."**

Forgiving like Jesus

For any Christian, the daily quest to be Christ-like

is ever-present. That doesn't mean we can reach the status of perfection Jesus has. It means we are to be 'like' Christ…as much like Him as we possibly can. That cannot exclude the whole action of forgiving others merely because so many people think it's nearly impossible to do. Now, if Jesus' mainstay, big title, major headline about Him were printed in the tabloids and social media hashtags today, it would be #Jesusforgives. Forgiveness is the major thread running through Christianity. It is THE good news of all good news. He forgave us. He died for us. He saved us. Many of us are readily willing and able to grasp hold of that truth. As overwhelming and soul-piercing as it is that He died because of us, we accept it and rejoice in it. Realistically, we see it as beneficial to us. Many of us have been taught throughout our lives to accept this truth and live as those who are forgiven, not as those who have fallen and have no way up.

1 John 1:9 says, **"If we confess our sins, he is faithful and just to forgive us our sins and to cleanse us from all unrighteousness."**

As part of the quest to be Christ-like, we're supposed to accept forgiveness as well as extend it to others. That reality is not one we embrace as readily as we do the one where we're forgiven of our own sins. This truth that we're to offer forgiveness is harder to accept. It's an action we have to take; not something we give others easily but we sure accept it when it's offered to us by Jesus. We have to do the work to forgive and often times it can be hard work. The Bible clearly states in **Matthew 6:14-15** that we must forgive others. It doesn't hint at it. It doesn't suggest it might be a good idea. It tells us we must forgive if we want to be forgiven. **"For if you forgive other people when they sin against you, your heavenly Father will also forgive you. But if you do not forgive others their sins, your Father will not forgive your sins."**

The quest to learn to forgive others is a great challenge for most of us. In talking to a youth group about forgiveness one time, concerning forgiving others, a young man told me, "Well, I'm not Jesus and He's part of the Trinity so He can walk on water and forgive people and all that miraculous stuff. It would take a miracle for me to forgive my stepdad for everything he's done to my family." My answer to him was, "Yes Jesus was perfect and He is part of the Holy Trinity. Jesus has abilities and capabilities we do not, however, if He asks us to do something, He will always, always give us the strength to do it and make a way for us to stand up under whatever load it is He wants us to carry. We also have access to God the Father, Jesus Christ, and the Holy Spirit to help us in the process of forgiveness. We aren't in this alone."

As I've found out over the years, almost all of us

feel the way this youth did at some point or another. In the moment my answer was a good one but it doesn't make the process of forgiving others any easier. Whether you're a teenager, a twenty-something, or an eighty-something, forgiveness is one of the hardest things we tackle on this Christian journey. Some things are done in an instant while others take a process. Growing closer to the Lord, being a student of His Word, and practicing forgiveness regularly is key to the act of forgiveness becoming second nature to a Christian.

When I feel as if I've failed at letting go of unforgiveness or it takes me longer to forgive than I know it should, I take solace in the words of Billy Graham. He said, "Being a Christian is more than just an instantaneous conversion - it is a daily process whereby you grow to be more and more like Christ."

Referencing **Ephesians 4:31-32,** if you look at the language there, it also tells us how we should be going forward, not just how we are to react in the present moment or towards past offenses. In other words, language in Ephesians is directed toward how we act and react in the present moment but also how we act and react in the future. It tells us to get rid of anger and every form of malice but also to "be kind and compassionate, forgiving each other". Forgiving is a reference to something that is ongoing, not just a one-and-done proposition. Forgiving each other, just as Christ forgave us is a perpetual act of obedience, not just something we're to do concerning one person, one occasion, or one offense.

What will it take?

The most important thing you can do to forgive and be able to say "It is finished?" and to make your forgiveness four hundred ninety and keep it four hundred ninety is to get out of your feelings! In **Ephesians 4: 32** it says that we should be tenderhearted or kind and compassionate to each other. It also says we should forgive each other just as Christ has forgiven us. Before you can be tenderhearted you have to do the work to let go of the negative feelings surrounding the transgression, the person, the hurt, and the pain you're trying to forgive.

Forgiveness has a whole lot to do with feelings. But we can choose the feelings we want to hold on to and those we want to release. It's really difficult to do when we're holding on to anger as our primary emotion. Anger easily takes over so many of our other emotions and becomes the predominant feeling we allow ourselves to feel. In other words, we begin to see everything through the eyes of anger, regret, and retaliation. That means we have to be determined and disciplined to reach in and reach up to find the strength to grasp hold of the truth about what forgiveness actually is. We have to combat the lies the enemy and the world tells us about what it says forgiveness is and what we should do about it to embrace what God's Word says about it.

So how do you stop living inside the feelings of anger and resentment you have when you feel offended and have been hurt or even when you feel you have hurt someone else? The answer, simple as it sounds, is to control your feelings by using the Word of God to redirect the repetitive thoughts and scenarios you hold on to that keep you seething inside. This is what worked not just for me but for so many people I've helped coach to release their anger, resentment, and frustration so they could release the grip of unforgiveness. By using Bible passages and quotes to redirect your thoughts, you're not just distracting your brain, although that happens as well, but you're retraining it to focus on the things that matter most and the truth of God's Word.

Three very practical ways to use the Word of God to help release those pent-up and repetitive feelings are:

#1 – Sit down with your Bible and look up passages that mean something to you; that matter to you and hit you straight in your heart. If you prefer to Google them or use an app on your phone, that's fine too. Just do it. Copy your favorites on index cards or on the back of business cards and make a small stack of them. Don't just write down Isaiah 41:13. Write down the actual words. Keep the cards with you at all times. Put one in your pocket in the morning and in your purse, on the dash of your car; on your desk at work, by the stove, and on the bathroom mirror. Every few days move the cards around and change them out so you don't become so used to them that you don't notice them any longer. Every time you start to seethe, you start to get angry or you start to go over and over that same old anger and resentment, read a scripture. Every single time. I mean every single time! Refocus your mind. It's important to add in some scriptures you might not have memorized because part of the redirection is the action of reading it from the card.

What I had to do in the beginning was also stop, close my eyes, and purposefully picture Jesus in my mind so I could calm down and focus. When I was angry and an obsessive resentful, retaliatory thought entered my head, there was no just grabbing a card to read a scripture at first. I had to focus on Jesus, pray, sing a worship song, stretch, and breathe before I could do it. Then I could read the card and let the words sink in. I would read it over and over until my brain let go of that unforgiving thought I was allowing myself to have and to feel. Afterward, I could move on with my day. I'd say from experience that it takes approximately twenty to thirty seconds to redirect your brain most of the time, that's it. It might take you ten minutes to get to the redirection part, to begin with, but it will become easier over time and with practice. In that ten to thirty seconds, however, you will have just derailed your unforgiveness from taking you down a ten, twenty, or thirty-minute road of building anger and resentment back up.

Grace was one thing I started to focus on the most, to begin with. I looked up scriptures dealing with grace. Remember, forgiving means ceasing to feel resentment, to pardon. Forgiveness and grace are direct relatives. Offering grace, which is that unmerited favor, is a good first step to walking in full Christ-like forgiveness.

#2 - Find quotes that you love about forgiveness and write those down. There may be several in this book that I've shared with you that will resonate. There are also some towards the back of this book in a section filled specifically with scripture and quotes to encourage you on your journey to let go. There are many quotes on the internet and in the Bible. Just be cautious not to write down the ones that encourage resentment and retaliation. Those kinds of quotes can also be found in abundance.

Make sure you choose quotes based in truth and encouragement. These are quotes you're going to read to yourself every single day until you don't need to read them anymore. They will become engrained in your daily thoughts. Some of these can be scripture as well, like **Ephesians 4:32** or **Isaiah 41:13**. Some of the quotes that helped me are serious and some are humorous because even though this is a serious topic that I'm very passionate about, I am all for using humor and joy in life as well.

Sounds simple, right? And it is, but it makes a huge impact on your brain. What you fill your mind with makes a difference and if you allow your mind to be filled with continual thoughts of pain, hurt, resentment, or revenge, you will stay immersed in it, and unforgiveness will continue to have a fierce grip on your life.

Helen

A woman named Helen told me one time that she couldn't stay focused enough at night when she was too overwhelmed and tired to read the scriptures she'd written down to try to switch her thought patterns so at night when she had issues with the anger threatening to take her over, keeping her awake and letting Satan attack her even more, she would listen to scripture through an app on her phone. Sometimes she would even play it while she fell asleep to keep herself from lying in bed and going over and over her hurt and pain. It worked well for her. It stopped her from spiraling down. She was a faithful, beautiful woman who struggled deeply for a few years with trying to forget and to forgive. Once she stopped trying to forget and put her energy and faith into simply forgiving, she was able to eventually forgive the man who took her only daughter's life as well as her grandchildren. That doesn't mean she condoned it. But by forgiving him, she was set free. She was set free from obsessive thoughts, anger, and unhealthy feelings of wanting to seek revenge, praying for God not to forgive him. Then and only then was she able to be tenderhearted just as the scripture tells us to be.

The journey that this precious woman of God took might seem impossible right now for you to go on but nothing God asks us to do is impossible. Not only was Helen able to forgive this man and get rid of her feelings of anger and resentment, but she was able to then fill that space where she'd carried that unforgiveness with the kind of feelings God wanted her to have. She became tenderhearted towards him and his family. While he is serving a life sentence in prison, his children are in need. Twice a month Helen takes his family food and gift cards, driving 3 hours to another state where they live to do so. By releasing the grip of unforgiveness and allowing herself to give grace, she found a place of tenderheartedness she never thought she'd be able to have. Living out amazing compassion through her forgiveness does not condone his horrible, sinful actions. She doesn't have to have him in her life to overflow with kindness towards his family and be an example to him and others. Within the space of grace, she found a kind of God-inspired tenderheartedness that helped heal her more than she could have ever imagined.

Helen brings me to **#3** – Turn your pain into purpose! Helen found a purpose through the pain she suffered. It was an immense, life-changing tragedy brought about by someone else's hands. She did the work it took to get out of her own feelings and become tenderhearted. In going through that process she found she had a big space in her life that had been previously taken up with unforgiveness and pain. She turned it into purpose. With time on her hands from her loss and no more obsessive thoughts of revenge fueling her up every day, she found a need to fill that space with something meaningful that honored God and her daughter and grandchildren.

Even if you haven't fully forgiven yet, turning your pain into purpose will help redirect your heart, mind, and soul and set you on the path to eventually embrace true forgiveness. There is no greater path to getting out of your own way than to get in the path of purpose. Go to your local church or community agency or a mission center and find out where you can plug in and find a purpose that will help take up the time, space, and energy you're currently using to stay trapped in unforgiveness and fueled by anger or resentment.

Woman of God, Let Go:

- I encourage you to intentionally muster up the effort it takes to forgive like Jesus; with grace and compassion. Yes, it takes work but the peace that comes from being able to lay your head down at night and truly rest is well worth it. More than that, the peace that comes from honoring God and what He told you to do in forgiving others and yourself is a kind of peace that lasts.
  1. Go through your previous chapter notes and choose some people/things you need to forgive. Don't take them on all at once. Just choose 2 or 3.
  2. Go through the steps in this chapter for each thing you need

to forgive. Pray and ask the Lord to show you what scriptures to write down and guide you to the quotes that will suit you best as you start this quest to systematically do the work you need to do in order to take your thoughts captive and release them from the grip of unforgiveness. Each time your mind goes off on a path of anger and obsessive thoughts about each of these you need to forgive, use the scripture and quotes you chose to help redirect your thoughts, and control which emotions you choose to feel.

- Looking at **2 Corinthians 10: 3-5** it says, **"For though we live in the world, we do not wage war as the world does. The weapons we fight with are not the weapons of the world. On the contrary, they have divine power to demolish strongholds. We demolish arguments and every pretense that sets itself up against the knowledge of God, and we take captive every thought to make it obedient to Christ."** Pray this out loud in your prayer time as often as you need to remind yourself that it is possible to take your thoughts captive and in doing so, you honor God.

- Remember, unforgiveness only has power over you as you let it. You can release the grip it has on your life and not make forgiving someone or something a one-time thing. Forgiveness should be a constant mindset that draws you closer and closer to being Christ-like. There is no other action, deed, thought, or way of life more Christ-like than that of living a life of perpetual forgiveness and tenderheartedness towards others.

- Serve! Find a place to serve; a place to turn your pain into purpose. Remember, there is no greater path to getting out of your own way than to get in the path of purpose. Start making calls and contacts this week, finding a place to put your time and energy.

*Writer and theological blogger Chris Sprinkle, for the Theology in the Raw blog, https://theologyintheraw.com/what-does-it-mean-to-become-more-like-jesus/

TRUE STORIES OF AMAZING FORGIVENESS

Arizona's story

Remember that woman I told you about from Arizona who hadn't forgiven her husband for cheating on her all those years? She and I spoke and prayed together in the women's restroom at a conference. Her health was horrible and yet they could find no physical underlying cause. Her therapist, her doctor, and even her pastor told her she had to forgive and let go. Unforgiveness had a mighty grip on her health. Her struggle to forgive her husband for cheating on her after so many years of marriage was only part of the issue. She struggled to forgive herself. After learning that he not only cheated on her with a woman at church but had been a serial cheater for most of their marriage, she didn't just feel betrayed by him; she felt she had betrayed herself. She felt ignorant, foolish, and embarrassed that she didn't know about any of her husband's unfaithfulness and addictions. Like many women who find out their spouse has cheated on them, she felt as if she couldn't trust her own instincts anymore. Perhaps she also felt like she couldn't trust God. After all, where was He in the middle of all this?

About a year after I'd been to that speaking engagement where I encouraged her to work hard to forgive and gave her some suggestions, including that she continue to go to therapy, she contacted me. I had prayed for her often but never knew what happened. She found my information online and reached out to me. I was overjoyed when she told me she found the key to forgiveness in the strength she gained from Jesus. Keeping her eyes on Him, deciding not to blame Him for her ex-husband's free will choices, and deciding that she wasn't to blame for someone else's choices either, freed her to finally forgive. It took her many months of practice in order to stop the obsessive thoughts and daydreams of retaliation but she did it. Like so many others I've spoken to, she also found a renewed sense of purpose and direction through serving others as a means of intentionally distracting herself from her incessant woeful thoughts and giving to those who needed her time and attention more than her unforgiveness did.

This beautiful woman worked hard to turn her life around and release the grip that unforgiveness had on her. She shared with me a quote that helped her and that same quote also eventually helped me. She said she came across it one day in a store. It was on a little plaque. The quote is by Malachy McCourt."Holding on to anger is like drinking poison and expecting the other person to die." She ended up using that quote, along with her favorite scriptures to remind herself that unforgiveness is toxic. It's not only toxic to your physical, mental, and emotional health but also to your spiritual health. The first step she took to release the grip of unforgiveness was to decide she wanted to. And so she did.

Helen's story

I've told you a little bit here and there about Helen. She's graciously allowed me to share her story in more detail. Helen is her middle name because she doesn't want her full name shared for privacy reasons but is happy for me to share her story in the hopes it helps someone else. The following events are disturbing but were shared by Helen so you can understand the fullness of what God was calling her to forgive. While she sincerely hopes no one else can relate to this, the reality is that on some level, there are more than a handful of people who can. In sharing her story she and I both hope that you will understand the various ways she had to forgive and also the misguided reasons she thought she thought at first that she needed to hold on to unforgiveness.

She hopes her story conveys the reasons that forgiveness is crucial to living a life of peace, joy, and obedience. Here is the scenario that forever changed her life:

<u>Summer 2011</u> - Helen had been waiting for her daughter to call. She hadn't heard from her and the call was past due by about 2 hours. She had a feeling in the pit of her stomach something was wrong. She was concerned. Red flags had been all over the place ever since her daughter had started dating Brody. Brody wasn't the first man in her daughter's life. Helen's daughter Kimmy had flitted from man to man when she was a teenager and into her early twenties. But she finally settled with a wonderful man when she was 26. He was a Christian who had a good head on his shoulders, was kind, and loved life. They married and had two children. One child was a girl who turned six years old in 2011 and a nine-year-old boy. Unfortunately, after 10 years of marriage, Brody was killed in a freak trucking accident. Kimmy hadn't been widowed long, yet in her grief, she decided to take up with a new man. Helen was not happy about it. First of all, Helen felt it was too fast and she knew Kimmy was still grieving, as were the kids. But Helen loved her daughter so she wanted to support her in every way she could.

Brody was not the kind of man Helen would have chosen for Kimmy. A few times in the past weeks Kimmy had called Helen crying. Though Kimmy didn't admit it, Helen suspected that Brody was getting violent. When she had her grandchildren with her the day before, they told her they were afraid of Brody. Helen talked to Kimmy when she dropped them back home. Helen felt prompted to tell her that she needed to get serious about getting away from Brody because if the kids were afraid of him there was a reason. Kimmy said that she loved him and she wanted to work things out but she was afraid of him and she was going to set some boundaries with him. Kimmy was supposed to see Brody the following morning so they could talk about their relationship. Helen was nervous for Kimmy but she knew the kids would be off to school and made Kimmy promise her that she would call her and fill her in on everything after she spoke with Brody.

That next morning Helen hadn't received a call yet from her daughter. It had already been 2 hours past when she thought Kimmy would call. Helen said she paced back and forth and was just about ready to grab her car keys to head over to check on Kimmy when the phone finally rang. The drive was only ten miles away but she was relieved to get the call and glad she wouldn't have to drive there. She picked up the phone and immediately heard Kimmy screaming. She was screaming for help. Helen ran and got in her car. The phone went dead. She dialed 911 immediately as she drove to Kimmy's house.

When she got to Kimmy's house she saw Brody dragging Kimmy down the driveway by her hair. Kimmy was a bloody mess. Helen got out of the car and immediately went after Brody. Brody dropped Kimmy and went after Helen. He ended up throwing Helen down a hill towards the ditch. He took off in his truck after that. Helen had hit her head and apparently passed out because when she came to she heard sirens. The police were already on the lookout for Brody after getting a description of his vehicle from a neighbor. Kimmy was dead and so we're both of the children.

When I talked to Helen a few years later and she shared her story with me she said, "Karen, I was so angry, of course. But I wasn't just angry at Brody and even angry at Kimmy for allowing him in their lives or just angry from the grief of losing my family. I was angry at God for allowing this to happen. I was angry at myself for not going over there earlier. There were a thousand 'what ifs' that went through my mind. But the thing that made me angriest was that I knew that one day if Brody confessed his sins, then God would forgive him and I didn't think he deserved forgiveness." Helen said, "I was also angry that God was going to command me to forgive. I know this because I've been a Christian inside and out from the time I was young. I always acted like forgiving was just a given and no big deal but I'd never had to forgive on this level, with this much pain and anger before. I didn't know how I was going to forgive. How would a righteous, loving God ask me to forgive someone who took my daughter and grandchildren from me? And I seriously believed that if I forgave him, I would be betraying my daughter and grandchildren."

Helen isn't alone in her thinking. We always hear how sin is sin and in the eyes of God, one sin equals another. In human courts, there are varying degrees of judgment and the sentencing is supposed to fit the crime. Sadly, I'm not sure that usually happens but we're told time and again that God is a just God and His ways are filled with wisdom. We know this but then to have to sit back and wait for God to apply the justice, much like us faithfully applying forgiveness to someone who has done something so atrocious and heart-breaking, is a whole different level of difficulty, bordering on nearly impossible.

As I listened to Helen telling me her story, my mind went right to where her thoughts had been years before. How could she forgive that? I'd think there would be some line within each of us that we feel we can't cross in order to forgive. I would think that when faced with something so extremely painful God would understand better than anyone else if we just can't bring ourselves to forgive. Helen and I discussed that very thing. I knew I was wrong and I recalled telling someone else years earlier the same thing. We still have to forgive, even when we think God will understand if we don't. Our feelings and perspectives don't change the meaning of God's Word. Of course, she reminded me of that very thing. The Word of God and His instructions about forgiveness are clear. If He asks us to do it, He will give us the way to do it. She shared with me one of the Bible verses that got her through some incredibly difficult and angry days on her journey to release the grip of unforgiveness. **1 Timothy 1:7, "For God has not given us a spirit of timidity, but of power and love and discipline."**

More than anything, after sitting in her unforgiveness for two full years, Helen realized what a chasm it had created between her and God. Her relationship with the Lord had dwindled down to barely a prayer a day and attending church only on special occasions. Her life-long faith and love for Jesus felt shallow and empty. She couldn't live that way any longer. When she woke up on Easter morning after that second year and realized that she didn't want to go to church, she flipped on the TV instead. When she did, she saw part of a passion play where Jesus was on the cross, hanging between the two thieves. When the actor playing the thief on the right said, "We deserve to die for our crimes but this man hasn't done anything wrong" she began to weep. It was a different kind of crying than she'd done before. She said it was from deep within. It was a mourning not just for her daughter and grandchildren but for the loss of the person she used to be before she let unforgiveness strangle the life out of her.

In that moment Helen realized that she was not the judge of Brody and just like him, she didn't deserve the forgiveness she got either. Who was she to deny what Jesus asked of her when she was a sinner too and Jesus' entire life and ministry were based on forgiveness? If she said she believed what the Bible said then she needed to live what the Bible said. I cried with Helen that day. But not because of sadness but because of the truth in her words and the beautiful glow on her face as she spoke so eloquently about the peace she found in her obedient decision to forgive, no matter what it took. They were tears of joy.

She told me that the truth is that forgiving others is an act of obedience and not forgiving is straight-out disobedience to God. It took time, but that finally sunk into her. She said it took a kind of discipline and self-control she didn't think she would be able to muster up but that same self-control could only come from Jesus and the amazing strength given to her through the Holy Spirit.

When talking to Helen as she shared her insights on forgiving, I have to admit that, that's when my real passion for sharing with others about forgiveness began as well. Praise God I didn't have such horrible tragedy perpetuated on my family like she did but the unforgiveness I had held on to against myself and others became more apparent the more I learned. In places I thought I had forgiven, I had not. That unforgiveness was no less toxic and no less a form of disobedience just because the transgressions seemed smaller than what Helen had endured. Just like the thief on the cross, I don't deserve a full pardon but yet Jesus chose to die for me, just as He chose to die for you and all those who come to Him.

The scripture Helen was referring to was from **Luke 23:39-43,** where it says, **"One of the criminals hanging beside him scoffed, "So you're the Messiah, are you? Prove it by saving yourself and us, too, while you're at it!" But the other criminal protested, "Don't you fear God even when you have been sentenced to die? We deserve to die for our crimes, but this man hasn't done anything wrong." Then he said, "Jesus, remember me when you come into your Kingdom." And Jesus replied, "I assure you, today you will be with me in paradise."**

My story

When I speak to women at conferences and retreats about forgiveness, I always share my own stories of forgiveness as well. After many weeks of prayer, I felt led to share some of that here as well. While I don't consider my story as amazing as Helen's story, or other stories similar to hers that I've heard over the years, it's my story and testimony nonetheless. I have a firm belief that telling my story, just like you telling your story, is what helps others to have victory over their unforgiveness and see that they too can forgive. With the help of the Lord and those who have come through something similar, everyone has the ability to be obedient and forgive. We also have the responsibility to tell others what He has done by forgiving us and then helping us to forgive others. **Psalm 105:1** says **"Give thanks to the LORD and proclaim his greatness. Let the whole world know what he has done."**

I previously shared with you that one of my favorite quotes is, "Holding on to anger is like drinking poison and expecting the other person to die." Your anger can become like a poison, slowly killing you from the inside out. I went through a time when I let my anger from unforgiveness slowly start to kill who I was and how I was called to live. It was killing my ability to tune into what God was saying and killing my ability to impart grace. The only thing I cared about grace during that time period was if I said grace at the table before I ate a meal. That's as far as it got.

In 2015, after years of major stress in my life from raising a special needs son whom I couldn't help the way I desperately wanted to help, and after many times of meltdowns, and verbal and physical assaults from him I was running low on grace. I had to give him grace and forgiveness though. Giving him grace had always been easier than others because he's a special needs adopted child. His IQ is lower. I am his comfort zone. I get all the good, all the bad, and all the over-the-top emotion he lets out. But as he got bigger and stronger it put me in danger. I finally had to work to put him in a psychiatric residential setting for a while until he could get into a group home where he could be safe and have support and socialization. On top of letting Satan tell me I was a failure as a parent, the stress, the years of home-schooling, fights, and fear added additional trauma to my life and my marriage in a tremendous way. It was all coming to a head in 2015.

During this same time period, my father was diagnosed with brain cancer. He passed away in November 2015. I was finally able to get intensive psychiatric help for my son in January

2016 and then I immediately started socking money away so I could afford to leave my husband. Though my husband had gotten therapy on and off for years, frankly, it was more off than on. He had what I would later find out was undiagnosed PTSD and trauma from incidents in his childhood and then from being a firefighter paramedic for twenty-four years. He had held children in his arms who died. He had seen crushed, mangled wrecks, overdoses, domestic violence, suicides and more. Sadly, like so many first responders in our country, the PTSD they endure is largely ignored while they're still working. I later found out that firefighters have the highest rate of divorce of any vocation in the United States. My husband's anger issues were immense and got worse as we dealt with the many life-long effects our son was enduring from being born to a birth mother who was an alcoholic and drug user.

My husband's PTSD came out in three ways. Yelling and screaming, pushing me, and checking out mentally and emotionally. Checking out was easiest for him because he was a workaholic. He constantly worked two or three jobs at a time. Most people thought I was a single mom. The sole responsibility for everything at the house, the bills, raising our adopted son, dealing with the doctors and therapists, getting him the special care he needed, and taking care of the household, was all on me. I was so tired. By the time 2015 rolled around our son didn't seem like our son anymore. He seemed like he was just mine. It was a position I never thought I'd be in.

2015 was the last year of my Dad's life here on earth. It was beautiful and so special. He kept his corny, fun sense of humor throughout. He never complained, no matter the pain. But for the last few weeks of his life, he was unable to talk. He was aware and would gesture and joke and whisper a little but mostly he spoke with his eyes. One day I was alone with him when my Mom went out to run some errands and so I was feeding him breakfast. He had a concerned look on his face. I asked him, "Dad, is something wrong?" He shook his head yes. I said "You look worried. Are you worried about Mom? She'll be back in a minute." He didn't like to be without her in the room. Even without being able to talk he always seemed to have his eyes on her. Even as weak as he was, when she came near his hospital bed, he would reach his hand through the bars of the hospital bed we set up in the house and pinch her on the butt.

When I asked my Dad again if he was worried about Mom he shook his head no. And he pointed at me. I said, "You're worried about me?" He shook his head yes. I said, "You don't have to worry about me Dad, I'm okay." He motioned for me to come closer and he whispered, "Be safe." Just a few weeks before that when he was still able to talk he made me promise him I would make sure I stayed safe. Safe from my son's violence and from my husband's issues. So, as he was lying there, his last few weeks of life, he wasn't worrying about his pain or the fact he couldn't eat much and he wasn't worried about his body dying. He was worried about me. It broke my heart. I didn't want him to spend any time or energy in his last days on earth worrying about me. I know if I had made different choices maybe he wouldn't be lying there worried about me. If I had been braver if I had stood up for myself more, if I had worked harder to find help earlier for my son... The "if I had's" are so hard to forgive within ourselves, aren't they?

I was blessed to be with my Dad when he passed away. I knew I would be. From the time it was apparent he wouldn't be with us much longer, I just knew God would allow me to be with him when he left this world. I'm so thankful. It's something I will never forget. But from that point forward I was determined to fulfill my promise to my Dad, no matter what.

When my Dad passed away my husband pretty much completely disappeared. In his grief and the reminders of his own father passing away, he decided to hide. Even on the day of the celebration of life, with so much going on and needing his support, he stayed for about an hour and then left. I was devastated and hurt. I needed support and he wasn't there to give it.

After Dad passed away and I was able to get my son into a residential placement, I started saving money to leave my husband. Every single day my anger grew. I was living off of that anger. Fueled by it. Letting it make all my decisions. I was angry at myself for letting myself be abused by our son and be neglected by my husband. But most especially I was angry at myself for letting my Dad worry about me. I was angry that I couldn't help my son, that I couldn't help my husband with his issues and I couldn't forgive myself for putting myself in that position in the first place. Some of it was my own fault and some of it not, but I still felt responsible for it all. I knew deep down that God had made us a family for a reason but I was angry about it all the same.

For an entire year after that, I saved every penny I could, all the while distancing myself more and more from my husband. It was a purposeful action and sometimes difficult to do because my husband was a nice man. He never, ever verbally abused me. He never berated me. He didn't talk down to me, and he would literally give the shirt off his back to anyone who needed it. He adored our son and his daughter. People loved my husband, and in my unforgiveness of him and myself, it made me even angrier. We became two strangers living in the same house. During that time he started to go to counseling more seriously than he had in the past. In fact, he was going every single week. But I didn't care anymore. He would ask me what he could do for me and I would tell him nothing. I didn't want him to do anything for me or anything with me.

I shared with maybe three or four people what I was doing and where I was mentally and emotionally and that I was going to leave him after filing for a divorce. I had been going to counseling for myself for two years. In light of all the many things going on, my Christian counselor, though he preferred that my husband and I try to stay married, was in complete support of me leaving him. After years of going to marriage and family counseling and my husband not sticking with it or individual counseling coupled with his rejection, the manifestation of his PTSD, and total emotional disconnection, I was more than ready to leave. By April 2017 I had saved a very large sum of money. I had a job with benefits and I was ready to disconnect. It was kind of an unspoken yet known concept between the two of us. He knew I was ready to leave, he just didn't know that I had already decided when. I was looking for a place to live and planned on leaving in May.

At the beginning of April, I was speaking at a church in Eastern Kentucky. It was a county-wide women's event with about 300 women. It was a beautiful, wonderful event. They'd asked me to talk to them about being still. I was up on the platform talking about what I'd learned about being still and how all the research I'd done about it pointed to the fact that being still was mostly about letting God have control when something amazing happened. I was standing there and suddenly it was as if I was stuck. I felt frozen in place. The words coming out of my mouth were about how we're supposed to step back and let God have control, that being still was actually a commandment, and that in the scripture that says "Be still and know", you must first be still (let God have control) in order to know. (to know anything He wants you to know). The irony of what I was trying to convey and how I had not been doing that in my own life hit me. While speaking, as animated as I usually am, I became extremely still. I just plain froze.

In an instant, it was as if fifteen buckets of water came crashing down on me. It woke me up. I looked up and I started to cry. I bawled. Three hundred women were looking at me, wondering what was going on, waiting for me to talk. In that moment I realized that I had not been letting God have control of anything in a very long time. I had made a promise to my Dad and so I was doing whatever I could to fulfill it, in the only way I knew how. But I did it without asking God to show me what it was He wanted me to do or how. I had taken full control, making up my mind what I was going to do without ever asking God. I had been making decisions without ever deferring to God to let Him control the way I would stay safe and what that might look like.

As I stood there and cried, I confessed to this entire group of hundreds of women that I was getting ready to leave my husband. I cried like I hadn't cried in a long time. I spoke from a depth of understanding I'd never had before and continued to lead the women in what would turn out to be an emotional, amazing event. Afterward, the Pastor of the church, who had been listening in at the back of the room approached me and said, "I have never seen anyone be so transparent, so overtaken by the Holy Spirit and moving before. This is what you were gifted to do. And I believe you need to pray more about what you're called to do with your marriage. I'll be praying for you and your husband."

After I went home that night, I sat up in the living and prayed. I actually listened to God. I hadn't done that in a long time. I knew then that I wasn't supposed to leave him. I was supposed to forgive him. So I prayed. I didn't know how I was going to do it but I just laid it all out to God. "Father, I don't want to stay here. I want to leave. But more than that I want Your will. I want my husband to be a man after your own heart, not to be perfect but to be seeking you to perfect him. I know I've made mistakes and I'm sorry. I know I made a promise to my Dad to be safe. But I haven't asked You to keep me safe, God. I'm thanking You now for keeping me safe and showing me what that means on this journey. And Lord, take this desire not to forgive from me. I say now, whether I feel it deeply or not, that I forgive him. And I forgive myself. Help me to continue to forgive and not take it back."

I went to bed that night after the conference and for the first time in years, I woke up the next morning without feeling angry. I woke up without the deep sadness that had been plaguing my life for the previous few years. By that same afternoon though, I wasn't feeling well. I just felt odd. My chest hurt, and my face was pale. I attributed it to being emotional. By that night my lips were turning blue. I asked my husband to take me to the ER. I found out I had pneumonia. I was running a fever of 103. I hadn't a clue! The doctor told me it would be three to four weeks for healing. I needed to make sure I didn't go to work, I didn't strain myself or overdo it, and I didn't need to be alone the first few days since I was going to be on lots of medication. As my husband and I were sitting there in the ER he said, "You heard what the doctor said, right?" I said, "Yes" and he said, "Well, I'll take the next few days off work." I told him I didn't need him to do that, I'd be fine. He just looked at me and said, "When are you going to let me take care of you?" I looked at him like he'd just spoken a foreign language." "What? What do you mean?" He said, "I'm here for you. I've been working hard for a year and a half to be here for you and you constantly push me away. I've been going to counseling every week for nearly two years. I'm going to church every week. I pray for you every day. You won't pray with me. I try to do the dishes and you won't let me. I ask if you need help with anything and you tell me no. You might feel okay right now but once this medication kicks in and this infection starts to break up, you're going to need someone to take care of you. When are you going to let me take care of you?"

Again it was like a bucket of cold water was thrown on me. I realized he was right. He had changed and I wouldn't acknowledge it. I had been so caught up in my anger and unforgiveness that I couldn't see the truth. At that point, it had been nearly four years since he'd exploded, yelled, or screamed. It had been a year since he had done more than work one job and for an entire year and a half he'd been going to counseling. But I never acknowledged any of it. I was sitting in the muck and mire of unforgiveness and I let it blind me. It had a tight grip on me in more than one way.

I learned that day that unforgiveness causes blindness. Forgiveness takes the scales off your eyes and opens your heart and mind to what God is doing. The obedience of forgiving others and yourself sharpens your discernment. But unforgiveness and anger blinded me from seeing what God was doing in the life of my husband. Unforgiveness kept me from seeing the reality that what I had been praying for, for so long, was happening. God's grace had enveloped my husband and I had pushed that grace away. I refused to see it. He was like Saul on the road to Damascus, seeing the light, having an intervention from Jesus, and becoming who we know as Paul. Yet, I couldn't see it because of the grip that unforgiveness had on me.

Here I was the one who was preaching to others about being still and letting God have control, yet I had taken that unforgiveness, fueled myself up with it, and pushed grace out of the picture. I had forgiven little things and some big things over the years and tried to just forget others but it never worked because I couldn't forget and when I would try to forgive I'd always taken that forgiveness back. After that day, I changed.

That day I found, through Jesus, my ability to give my husband grace. I gave unmerited, unearned, divine assistance and favor. After all that had happened, in my mind, he didn't deserve forgiveness. He had emotionally abandoned me. He had checked out and used his anger to distance himself. That was the worst part to me. He didn't deserve grace but then again, neither did I. We gave it anyhow. And that's what Jesus does for us.

I found that if I sought Jesus' help then I had more than enough grace for him and for myself. Through that grace, God changed everything. In 2022 my husband and I celebrated our twentieth anniversary. I love spending time with him. We laugh a lot. He works one job. We pray together every single day. We do Bible study together. And yes, he took care of me during that bout of pneumonia and I let him. He's helped me in many ways since then, and I've continued to let him. We work hard to give each other the grace that any marriage, and every relationship so desperately needs. When we forgive, it absolutely has to be a seventy times seven, 490 type of forgiveness. There's no sneaking in and stealing it back in the middle of the night because I had a dream he did something that ticked me off. There's no taking back the forgiveness because he fell asleep in the movie theater when we were supposed to be on a date. If I've had a bad day and I'm grumpy, he doesn't get to withhold grace from me either.

I learned that for me, grace is the first thing I had to embrace in order to practice "Keepin' it 490!" I also learned that this 490 type of forgiveness takes grace but it also takes humbleness. Whether you're trying to forgive someone else or working on forgiving yourself, it takes being humble.

Colossians 3: 12 tells us that, "**Therefore, as God's chosen people, holy and dearly loved, clothe yourselves with compassion, kindness, humbleness, gentleness and patience.**"

The definition of humble is "having or showing a modest or low estimate of one's own importance. Unassuming, free from vanity. Not proud or haughty: not arrogant." * I rarely quote from the message translation of the Bible because it doesn't usually resonate with me but this modern version in current language kind of spoke to me in this instance. **Ephesians 4:2-3** talks of Paul, locked up in a cell because he was a disciple and follower of Jesus. **"In light of all this, here's what I want you to do. While I'm locked up here, a prisoner for the Master, I want you to get out there and walk, better yet, run - on the road God called you to travel. I don't want any of you sitting around on your hands. I don't want anyone strolling off, down some path that goes nowhere. And mark that you do this with humbleness and discipline—not in fits or stops and starts, but steadily, pouring yourselves out for each other in acts of love, alert at noticing differences and quick at mending fences."**

That humble position of just releasing unforgiveness out of obedience is so important. Who are we to say that we are too good to forgive someone else or that someone else is not worthy enough to be forgiven when we are the same as them? If anyone could say they are too good to give another person forgiveness, it would have been Jesus Christ. But He didn't. He died for the forgiveness of all who accept Him, not just some of us. One of the most quoted scriptures from the Bible tells us that He died for "who so ever". **John 3:16: "For God so loved the world that he gave his one and only Son, that <u>who so ever</u> believes in him shall not**

perish but have eternal life."

My husband and I are amongst the who so ever. Are you? My hope and prayer is that you are.

Woman of God, Let Go:

- I encourage you to read the verses in **Luke 23: 26-49** and remember or perhaps learn for the first time, how Jesus died all in the name of forgiveness. That forgiveness is for all who come to Him, repent and accept it. He is our example, our strength, our Rock, and our Redeemer. Allow Him to be.

- If you haven't released the grip of unforgiveness, perhaps you're in a position similar to where I was in needing to immerse yourself in the truth of grace and humbleness. Find scripture that points you to true grace and humbleness as shown in God's Word. Write it down, pray over it, and ask God to change your heart to one that embraces grace and start your forgiveness journey over with a humble heart.

- Are you walking around with scales on your eyes? Blinders? Are you unable to see how God is moving or what He's doing in your life or perhaps in the life of someone you've refused to forgive? Pray and ask

Him to remove your blinders, giving you greater discernment and the ability to see people through His eyes, rather than your own.

- Do you have a story of forgiveness to tell? Write it down, or record it. Share it with others. I believe Jesus is calling us to share with others our stories of forgiveness. Let your forgiveness of others and yourself be a part of your testimony, for there is no greater witness to living a Christ-like life than to do as Christ did and forgive. Living in a world that tells us to forgive and forget or to seek revenge and get even, we're sorely lacking in the true stories of successful forgiveness. In sharing your story, simple or complex, deeply personal or painful, consistent or exhausting, you may help someone else who is struggling to forgive.

I encourage you, as you walk in obedience, claiming victory over the grip of unforgiveness in your life, to reach back and help someone else through that same journey to let go.

*Miriam Webster

SCRIPTURE, QUOTES AND ENCOURAGEMENT FOR YOUR JOURNEY

When I started speaking at conferences about forgiveness and leading women's retreats specifically about not letting unforgiveness steal your peace, I would always come out with a nice mixed bag of quotes I love on the topic. If you listen to any of my episodes on The Woman Inspired Podcast, you'll notice that I start each episode with a quote, or as I have coined them, "podquotes". (Nothing fancy, just simply a meshing of podcasting and quoting.)

I find quotes, be they directly from the Word of God or by theologians, historians, artists, profound thinkers, or the average everyday person, that are affirming and thought-provoking. I like to share them with others. Wisdom comes in all kinds of packages, ages, shapes, and sizes. For me, a well-memorized or repeated quote and Bible verse can have a profound effect on guiding my day and shaping my thoughts. I share these with you in hopes that you'll also make a list of your own for current and future encouragement and to share with others.

From the Word of God

May these words of my mouth and this meditation of my heart be pleasing in your sight, LORD, my Rock, and my Redeemer. **Psalm 19:14**

And without faith, it is impossible to please God, because anyone who comes to him must believe that he exists and that he rewards those who earnestly seek him. **Hebrews 11:6**

Do not conform to the pattern of this world, but be transformed by the renewing of your mind. Then you will be able to test and approve what God's will is - his good, pleasing, and perfect will. **Romans 12:2**

Be kind and compassionate to one another, forgiving each other, just as in Christ God forgave you. **Ephesians 4:32**

If we confess our sins, he is faithful and just and will forgive us our sins and purify us from all unrighteousness. **1 John 1:9**

For if you forgive other people when they sin against you, your heavenly Father will also forgive you. But if you do not forgive others their sins, your Father will not forgive your sins. **Matthew 6:14-15**

On justice and judgment

Consequently, just as one trespass resulted in condemnation for all people, so also one righteous act resulted in justification and life for all people. For just as through the disobedience of the one man the many were made sinners, so also through the obedience of the one man, the many will be made righteous. **Romans 5:18-19**

Love and faithfulness meet together; righteousness and peace kiss each other. Faithfulness springs forth from the earth, and righteousness looks down from heaven. **Psalm 85:10-11**

Righteousness and justice are the foundation of your throne; love and faithfulness go before you. **Psalm 89:14**

God "will repay each person according to what they have done." To those who by persistence in doing good seek glory, honor, and immortality, he will give eternal life. But for those who are self-seeking and who reject the truth and follow evil, there will be wrath and anger. There will be trouble and distress for every human being who does evil: first for the Jew, then for the Gentile; but glory, honor, and peace for everyone who does good: first for the Jew, then for the Gentile. For God does not show favoritism. **Romans 2:6-11**

About obedience

"Therefore everyone who hears these words of mine and puts them into practice is like a wise man who built his house on the rock. The rain came down, the streams rose, and the winds blew and beat against that house; yet it did not fall, because it had its foundation on the rock. But everyone who hears these words of mine and does not put them into practice is like a foolish man who built his house on sand. The rain came down, the streams rose, and the winds blew and beat against that house, and it fell with a great crash." **Matthew 7:24-27**

If you keep my commands, you will remain in my love, just as I have kept my Father's commands and remain in his love. I have told you this so that my joy may be in you and that your joy may be complete. My command is this: Love each other as I have loved you. Greater love has no one than this: to lay down one's life for one's friends. You are my friends if you do what I command. **John 15:10-14**

Blessed is the one who does not walk in step with the wicked or stand in the way that sinners take or sit in the company of mockers, but whose delight is in the law of the LORD, and who meditates on his law day and night. **Psalm 1:1-2**

Do not merely listen to the word, and so deceive yourselves. Do what it says. Anyone who listens to the word but does not do what it says is like someone who looks at his face in a mirror and, after looking at himself, goes away and immediately forgets what he looks like. But whoever looks intently into the perfect law that gives freedom, and continues in it—not forgetting what they have heard, but doing it, they will be blessed in what they do. **James 1:22-25**

Encouraging quotes:

The goodness you receive from God is a treasure to share with others. – Elizabeth George

Don't judge other people more harshly than you want God to judge you. – Marie T. Freeman

When you are weary and everything seems to be going wrong, you can still utter these four words: "I trust You, Jesus." – Sarah Young

The steady discipline of intimate friendship with Jesus results in men becoming like Him. – Harry Emerson Fosdick

God is interested in developing your character.

At times He lets you proceed, but He will never let you go too far without discipline to bring you back. In your relationship with God, He may let you make a wrong decision. Then the Spirit of God causes you to recognize that it is not God's will. He guides you back to the right path. — Henry Blackaby

It hurts when God has to PRY things out of our hands! — Corrie Ten Boom

"Forgiveness is a powerful expression of the love within our soul." - Anthony Douglas

"Forgiveness is above all a personal choice, a decision of the heart to go against the natural instinct to pay back evil with evil." - Pope John Paul II

"To forgive is to set a prisoner free and discover that the prisoner was you."- Lewis Smedes

"In the shadow of my hurt, forgiveness feels like a decision to reward my enemy. But in the shadow of the cross, forgiveness is merely a gift from one undeserving soul to another."-Andy Stanley

Throughout my journey to become more Christ-like in my thoughts and actions, I have learned that the most Christ-like thing I could ever do would be to forgive others. - Karen McCracken

ABOUT THE AUTHOR

Karen McCracken is the author of several books, including her 2023 Amazon Best-Selling book, Woman Stand Firm. She is also a Christian speaker and comedian who has spoken at over 350 women's conferences and retreats across the United States.

Karen hosts The Woman Inspired Podcast and was nominated for 3 Spark Media Podcasting awards. Her passion is to reach women inside and outside the church setting with the gospel message and to come alongside women in the Body of Christ with the message of hope and truth for those who feel lonely, afraid, and are drowning in an ever-changing, frightening world.

Karen is a wife, mom, avid gardener, and loves the outdoors. She's handy in the kitchen, loves to dance while she does housework, and enjoys making other people laugh.

To tune in to Karen's podcast, go to womaninspired.com or look for The Woman Inspired Podcast on your favorite podcast platform.

Other books by Karen McCracken

5 Stars for the best-selling
Woman Stand Firm
Armor Up in the Battle for Your Identity

5.0 out of 5 stars - WOW! This book is a MUST read for EVERY woman! 9/23/23

"From the introduction to the last page this book outlines the challenges that ALL Christian women encounter, but more importantly Karen defines the who, what and why's of how the armor of God will lead you to God's will and help YOU realize who God made you to be."

5.0 out of 5 stars - Phenomenal work! 9/18/23

Woman Stand Firm is a phenomenal work. Karen has so clearly poured her heart as well as her contagious sense of humor into each chapter...Each page is dripping with "chicken soup" for the soul-like having a conversation over coffee with a close friend. If you are looking for encouragement and a clearer understanding of who you are in Christ, I implore you to find yourself wrapped up in these pages.

Karen begins by calling out the lies and labels society so readily places on today's woman, and strips them away while placing you lovingly at the throne of the one who created you. Karen then takes a deep dive into our true role and identity in Christ our king, and shows not just the suggestion of how to view the armor of God, but the command we have to be warriors protected by God's word in his truth and righteousness imputed to our account.

5.0 out of 5 stars - Insightful and thought provoking 9/19/23

Whether you are a new Christian or one who's had a relationship with God for years, this book will help you to look at scripture in a new way. Karen presents the Armor of God in a manner that all women can relate to. It helps you gain a deeper understanding of scripture and helps you relate it to your life. I would recommend this for any and all women seeking to deepen their relationship with God. I plan on sharing this with my daughter as well as the ladies in my Sunday School class. Excellent read!

<u>NOTES</u>

KAREN MCCRACKEN

WOMAN LET GO

KAREN MCCRACKEN

Made in the USA
Las Vegas, NV
16 January 2025

16523720R00095